and mamma

happy birthday

TO EVERYTHING
A SEASON

TO EVERYTHING A SEASON

A YEAR IN ALBERTA RANCH COUNTRY

MARILYN HALVORSON

Stoddart

First published in 1991 by
Stoddart Publishing Co. Limited
34 Lesmill Road
Toronto, Canada
M3B 2T6

CANADIAN CATALOGUING IN PUBLICATION DATA
Halvorson, Marilyn, 1948–
To everything a season

ISBN 0-7737-2540-7
1. Ranch life – Alberta. I. Title.

FC3670.R3H3 1991 636'.01'0971233 C91-094807-0
F1076.H3 1991

Cover Design: Leslie Styles
Printed in the United States of America

To the memory of my dad,
Trygve Halvorson,
and of my uncle,
Ed Halvorson

Because they loved this land

Preface

"Land is the only thing in the world that amounts to anything, for 'tis the only thing in this world that lasts. 'Tis the only thing worth working for, worth fighting for—worth dying for....

"And to anyone with a drop of Irish blood in them the land they live on is like their mother."

Those words, from another time and another place, and spoken to Scarlett O'Hara by her father, exist only in the mythical pages of *Gone with the Wind*. But just as truth is stranger than fiction, fiction may be truer than truth. Because I can find no better words to express the way I feel about the land. To me, the land, and all the wealth of life it supports, is as precious as life itself. But then, I *am* half Irish.

I live and work on the same 640 acres of land where I grew up and where my dad homesteaded some sixty years ago. When he died twelve years ago it seemed only natural for me to keep the cow-calf operation going. The ranch, about seventy miles northwest of Calgary, is nine miles from the nearest town, Sundre (population approximately 2,000), where I teach high school half time. Except for one open quarter section a couple of miles down the road, this land is mainly forest. Spruce and poplar, mostly, with hay fields carved out here and there.

This isn't an efficient ranch. Since I have neither a set of modern haying equipment nor much expertise in the art of keeping complex equipment running, my hay is out on shares. (A friend uses his equipment to cut and bale the hay and in return gets half of the crop.) This means I can winter only half as many cattle as the land could otherwise support. Also, land that is covered with trees doesn't grow much grass. Of course, the efficient thing to do would be to clear off the trees. But efficiency isn't what really matters to me.

For me, to live on the land is to live with the land, to become a part of the ever-changing yet never-changing pattern of the seasons. It is to accept the bounty the land freely gives but to accept it as just that, a gift, and not to destroy the Earth itself in our greed to take more and more.

It is to remember that while we may be the smartest species, we have much to learn about being the wisest. We must learn to accept a place in the scheme of nature as humbly as the smallest insect does, and to realize that only by living in harmony and generosity with the rest of nature can we truly share in the magnificence of the world as God created it.

Too often we seem to feel that only in a life of speed and complexity can we find challenge and fulfilment. In fact, only yesterday I was discussing the illusive Canadian identity with my grade 10 social studies class and we came upon a quote in which someone had chosen "simplicity" as a word to describe the Canadian lifestyle. Instantly, the kids took offence. "We are not simple people!" they bristled.

Maybe they are right. But if they are, I believe it is to their and our loss. Henry David Thoreau called on the people of his time to "simplify, simplify!" I think the message is still good today. We live so fast that we never see the world around us.

This is a journal of simplicity, of a year spent opening my eyes, my ears—and my heart—to the world in which I live, the forested foothill cattle country of Alberta. It is a journal of the simple pleasures, and the pain, the contentment and the misery, that make up one year in a life on the land. It is not a record of the sweeping events that flash across the TV news at six o'clock; it is a record of moments, images that come and go, often witnessed by no one else, and made infinitely more valuable by their fleeting quality. It is a journal of birth and death, warmth and cold, planting and harvest—and it bears witness once again to the ageless truth of the words of Solomon, "To everything there is a time and a season . . . ."

Seasons are strange and arbitrary things. Who says that the year is neatly divided into three-month sections like a well-cut apple pie? Whoever invented this arrangement did not live in the Alberta foothills, where March, our first official spring month, often finds us frozen solid and April showers usually come in white-flake form. But this is also the country where Christmas can find us with water running down the roads and where our beloved chinook can raise temperatures sixty Fahrenheit degrees overnight. This really is the true North, strong and *free*, a land which breaks the rules and follows no patterns.

I, too, am a rule-breaker. Logical people start journals at the beginning of a year, or at least at the beginning of the month. Mine begins on the tenth of September, because it was then that the idea hit me.

September 10

Today is the tenth, a sunny Sunday with blinding brilliance in the blue of the sky and dazzling diamonds in the wet grass. A day of smiling sun, teasing an earth that felt the first sharp bite of frost overnight. The beans and zucchinis are gone, the potato tops turned to black-green slime, making me more willing to dig beneath them than when digging meant first ripping out a lush green top.

Still, summer is not in full retreat. Asters and petunias bloom on undeterred, now visited by slow-waking bumblebees who need until late afternoon to shake the lethargy of the frosty night from their cold-blooded bodies. They bumble past me now as I sit on the sun-hot deck against the south side of the house, occasionally fumbling in their flight and causing me some concern that one may stumble down my neck. There is no more placid creature, but still, a bee down the neck is not a happy bee.

Dragonflies, too, have reawakened. They skim across the lawn like irridescent airplanes with loudly clicking propellers. I wish them good hunting for, of course, the hardy mosquitoes will still be around.

The yard is alive with birds. Little yellow warblers, a kind I've never seen before, are stealing my chokecherries. For a while, with typical human avarice, I thought maybe I should hurry and pick the cherries before they were all gone. But then I thought again. Did I really want to get involved with jelly-making? No, not half as badly as those birds wanted to get involved with cherry-eating! Besides, which is worth more? A jar or two of gummy jelly or a couple of afternoons spent watching the little yellow birds partying on my lawn?

The juncoes are here, flocking around the house, one sure sign of summer's end. They're a rather foolish little bird, all dressed up in their twin white tail feathers but not paying much attention to the traffic rules. As I sit here, one tries to fly through the big front window and bounces off, unhurt. A cheap lesson about windows which I hope he took to heart.

I found one tell-tale feather on the carpet this afternoon. Evidence that one of the cats had fowl for lunch? Maybe. I hope not, but if he did, I will be sad for the bird but I won't be angry at the cat. He was born a predator and no amount of civilization can erase the instinct that says "Pounce!" when a careless lunch happens by. As someone (Mark Twain, I think) once said, "I pass judgement on no animal but man." Animals do what they do because they know no better. Man knows much better but he does it anyway.

SEPTEMBER 11

It froze again last night, harder than the night before, but we are already on borrowed time in this country. Anytime after mid-August is fair game for frost. But even frost has its rewards. The air seems changed, purified by cold.

August began with muggy, hazy days, air like lukewarm soup, and edgy glances at the sky as weathermen gave forth weather watches and reports of funnel-cloud sightings. Since the 1987 Edmonton tornado, which was supposed to have developed in the foothills not far from here, we haven't been quite so smug about our nonviolent summer weather.

Then, from mid-August on, we were caught in a cycle of showers, major rain, sun and back to showers. Like a dog chasing its own tail, the weather couldn't seem to get straightened out and on the road again. Even now, hay cut in early August lies in long, dark, sullen snakes of windrows—a month's excellent winter feed turning into slime.

But now we're going to get some sunshine.

SEPTEMBER 13

Late August and early September is the time of the air currents. I don't know the exact scientific reason and I don't want anyone to spoil the magic for me by drawing lines on a weather map, but on early fall evenings, the air seems to lie in layers or pockets, some warm, some cold.

One of the most lasting memories of my teenage years is of riding in the dusk, galloping, of course, sweeping through the cool evening air, feeling almost too cold, and then suddenly being engulfed by the comforting softness of summer-warm air. It was like being wrapped in the reassuring arms of Mother Nature herself. Then, a second later, the warmth was gone, replaced by a pocket of sharp autumn air. Warm, cold, warm again. You could ride for miles on that temperature roller coaster, an exhilarating, senses-tingling high—legal and free. I feel sorry for kids who spend their time looking for "kicks" and never find the magic that is out there, free for the taking, in the real world.

The air currents are still there. I find them once in a while and, instantly, I'm back there, riding my Goldie horse, who now gallops only in the sky, and reliving my teenage years—ghost years on a ghost horse . . .

SEPTEMBER 14

I walked in the pearly dawn this morning and watched the sky change from gray to mottled rose-gray, to rose-blue, and finally to blue. The air was still and gentle. No bite of frost today.

The dog came with me, of course, and we met The Prince pussyfooting through the corral. When he saw I was walking away, not home for breakfast, The Prince jumped onto a fencepost and sat complaining until I came back, swooped him onto my shoulder and carried him home.

Then, he wasn't hungry. The liar had already dined out.

This afternoon, I sit on the deck in shorts and tank top, absorbing the heat. Better to take all there is now during these Indian summer days. Winter will come too soon and stay too long.

As I try to write, Missy comes to help me. Her idea of help is to flop her head in my lap—never mind that my notebook is already there—and stare soulfully into my eyes for as long as I will put up with it.

I never meant to own a Missy dog. I went for nearly a year without a dog after Stormy, our big old shepherd, died; I didn't really miss having a pair of reproving brown eyes fill me with guilt every time I drove away from the yard. But Missy was a charity case. A stray that showed up at a neighbor's place one weekend. They already had a dog and were making regretful noises about having to do away with the stray, followed by thoughtful pauses and, "But you don't have a dog now, do you, Marilyn?" What could I do? When you have the power to save a life, you can't just turn away. So, I acquired a Missy dog.

A purebred Heinz kind of dog. If I had to hazard a guess, I'd say mainly Border collie and Irish setter—color and markings from the former, body and brains from the latter. She can run all day, tops out at well over thirty miles per hour, and leaps in and out of the truck box ten times a day for exercise. But dumb! Well, maybe not entirely dumb, but not entirely trainable either. She disobeys. I scold her. Mainly, she smiles. Sometimes she rolls over. Sometimes, if she does something really dangerous, such as chasing cars, I spank her. She accepts it. Makes no effort to get away, no effort to fight back. She just accepts it with a look that says, "Go ahead, if you have to hit me, hit me. I won't hold it against you. But I was just doing what I had to do and I'll do it again next time I get the chance. That's the way I'm made . . ."

I don't punish her much any more.

So, she lays her big mug on my lap and interrupts my work and I forgive her. Anyone who can stare into my eyes with a look that says, "You're the most beautiful, charming, intelligent, admirable person in the whole world" deserves a little patience.

SEPTEMBER 15

This is the time of the striped grass, yellow with a thousand other colors edged along it. It stands tall and wind-rippled along the sides of the road like jungle grass I've seen in pictures. I can't help half expecting—and half wishing—to spot a tiger crouched in its perfect camouflage.

This is supposed to be the last nice day for a while. Cooler with showers tomorrow, then colder with rain or snow on Sunday. And my August-cut hay still lies, now newly turned, in ever-blacker windrows stretched across the grown-up field. The rest of the hay and the green feed are down now, almost dry enough to bale. But I'm afraid close doesn't count. If not today, then when will be the next chance to get it baled? There's only half enough for winter in bales so far. Will this be the year when, with a bumper crop rotten and buried beneath the snow, I have to buy feed?

It has looked this bad other years but we've always managed. I guess that's what faith is all about. Knowing that, although Alberta is a hard country that likes to scare us once in a while, it has never really let us down.

I walked a little later than usual this evening but I didn't miss a thing—or if I did, I made up for it by seeing a lot of things I would have missed earlier. Things like a small brown toad, sitting almost totally camouflaged among the fallen leaves; only the thin yellow stripe down his back gave him away.

I wondered what was on his little toad mind as he sat there with that expression shared by toads and a certain breed of university professors.

It's getting cool for cold-blooded critters to be out. How does a toad decide when it's time to burrow into the mud and get away from it all for a few months? How can they stay alive down there? I wouldn't believe that they actually can had I not seen the evidence myself one day in early spring. Sitting sluggishly in the mud beside the newly thawed beaver dam was the skinniest frog I've ever seen. With his hipbones protruding at all angles he looked like an appeal for famine relief. The sight of him, obviously a frog who hadn't had a square meal in months, convinced me. Amphibians really do hibernate.

The kingfisher was out tonight, chittering to himself as he skimmed above the beaver dam, dipping suddenly to catch I-don't-know-what—I don't think there are fish in the dam. I would like to know this kingfisher better but he never stays for long. I don't think he's really wild, just too busy for chitchat.

I had a lesson in despair at the dam tonight. Despair was a dragonfly who had skimmed too low across the water, wet his wings and been pulled down into the water. Now he tried to take off again, but the water would not let him go. I wanted to reach out to him with a branch but he was too far out.

"Too far out." The words remind me of the lines from the Stevie Smith poem, "Not Waving but Drowning," about the boy who always did crazy things to attract attention and whose drowning cries for help were ignored. "But he was too far out and not waving but drowning."

Like him, and like the dragonfly, it seems that, at times, we all get a little too far from shore.

Though nature can be cruel, she will not take without giving in return. Hope walks hand in hand with despair. I met it on the creek bank as well. There stood a grove of young balsam poplars, shedding their colored leaves and preparing for the death season ahead. But as I looked more closely at the trees, I made a discovery. Beside each dying, falling leaf was a leaf bud, sticky and tightly curled but as complete and perfect a leaf as it will be next May. Surely this is hope—and faith. A tree not yet stripped of this year's leaves, with eight months of fall and winter ahead of it, yet ready and waiting for that first warm week in May.

If winter comes can spring be far behind?

SEPTEMBER 17

When people ask me when I'm going to write a novel for grownups, I say, "When I grow up." It's true. I really have never grown up. I proved it again today.

After a four-hour drive back from Medicine Hat in the rain, I was in need of some "real" air. It stopped raining about five so I went out for one of my explorations across the road. It's wonderful out in that wild quarter. Once you're out of sight of the road you might as well be in the wilderness of Alaska, it's so untouched.

It was beautiful there today. The clouds hung heavy and dark, yet the woods were lit by yellow poplar leaves, bright chandeliers in the gloom.

Maybe it was those bright trees that made me do something really un-grownup. I got lost—as lost as you can get in a quarter section, fenced on four sides! I must have taken the brightness in the trees as sunshine and headed "west" into the late-afternoon sun. How else could I have managed to go west, toward home, and end up at the *north* fence!

But that wasn't my most immature act of the day. That came as I tried to tiptoe carefully through a swamp, stepping on only the high spots. Unfortunately, I hit a low spot, and filled my brand-new, no-leak rubber boots with liquid mud.

It started to rain again, and since I was a long way from home, on the wrong side of the swamp and lost, I got soaked to the skin. I was one bedraggled camper by the time I got home.

SEPTEMBER 18

As he always does when I weaken and let him stay in at night, The Prince rose at five A.M. and scratched the best chair to get my attention. That was part of the training process when he was a kitten. That is, he trained me. It all started logically enough. He scratched the chair. For punishment I dumped him outside. That happened two or three times. Then, one day he wanted out. He went to the door but I didn't notice him in the first ten seconds. He went over and started scratching the chair. *That,* I noticed. Out he went. From that day on, he's gone directly to chair-scratching whenever he wants out—even at this unearthly hour. Where did I go wrong, Pavlov?

It was beautiful outside. A gray sky full of stars and an almost-full moon, a surprise when the forecast had threatened snow. The air was warm and soft. The frost came later, turning the grass crunchy by seven.

SEPTEMBER 19

I walked in the first light this morning and the sky was made of baby blankets, all gentle pink and blue, with a white daytime-moon floating there.

As I crossed the barnyard The Prince came galloping to meet me, his wonderful tail straight up and fluffed out like a chimney brush. I have a friend who calls him Flagstaff. Missy saw The Prince coming and took after him. They chased each other for a while. The Prince skipped reading the part of the rule book that says dogs chase and cats run. By his interpretation, a cat runs ten feet, turns around and chases the dog twenty feet. Missy agrees to these rules. Her black rubber nose has met The Prince's claws before.

And so they play, with wicked innocence. Two young children of the universe, free, and a little crazy with the joy of just being alive.

It is the time of the golden leaves. As I walk, the breeze rustles through the drying leaves, making a sound like falling rain. The leaves fall like raindrops, too, in sudden golden showers.

Leaves die like people. Some hang on and on, though they've shrivelled and turned gray. Others go out in a blaze of glory, still golden and shining, but nonetheless losing their grip on this life and sailing into a new dimension.

The ground is drifted with golden coins, so beautiful but so soon doomed to decay. Nature seems so wasteful. She creates a billion, billion perfect leaves, turns them to gold, then throws them away. Millions of beautiful kittens and puppies—even babies—are born into a world that doesn't need them, a world where their lives are of no value and they are doomed to short and miserable lives. Why can't nature make just a few of the beautiful things and take proper care of them?

SEPTEMBER 20

As I walk along the edge of the beaver dam I keep hearing sudden little PLOPS. Whenever I look in the direction of the sound all I see is a little fountain of water and a big air bubble. Eventually, I catch on. The PLOPS are muskrats, their diving turning the dam into a bubbling volcano, a simmering pot of chocolate pudding. Or maybe just a boiling batch of lip-smacking muskrat stew.

SEPTEMBER 21

I wasted ten minutes this morning just holding The Prince. No, that's not right. I didn't waste the time. I invested it in my mental health.

A cat is a psychiatrist. When you're all wired up, tense and worried, and getting ulcers, he jumps onto your lap. Immediately, he begins therapy. First he shows you how to relax. Every inch of his body goes limp, so relaxed he seems almost to sink into you, warming and comforting your innermost being. Then he begins to purr. Those gentle, regular vibrations seem so effortless. Already you are becoming drowsy. Then he studies your face with those green, green eyes, bottomless pools of sea water that wash into your very soul, understanding you completely, accepting you.

Slowly, ever so slowly, those eyes grow sleepy. The lids flutter down, once, twice... The cat breathes one deep sigh of perfect content. He is asleep.

And so are you.

SEPTEMBER 22

Yesterday was one of those perfect fall days that make you want this season to last forever. There was only one problem. I had to teach until eleven, then return to town for a meeting from two-thirty to four-thirty, and then come back for *another* meeting from seven to eight-thirty.

But at least I managed to live a little in between captivities. At four-fifteen I looked at those poor full-time teachers who hadn't seen the light of day since eight A.M. and thought about what they had missed.

Our society is crazy. Pursuing "the important business" of life we miss out on the real business of *living*—like walking out into a golden day that will never come again.

Today I was sixteen again. It was one of those perfect fall days, with golden leaves, blue skies and a warm, wild wind. I was a rebel this afternoon and, instead of doing housework, yardwork, schoolwork or even bookwork, I took the Copper colt out for a ride. He's just about broke now, but superstition hangs a little heavy over me. It was just about a year ago that I also thought he was "just about broke." That was the day that, so fast I never quite knew how it happened, I was broke and he wasn't! I spent the next six weeks with my right wrist in a cast, still trying to figure out what happened. Still, I shouldn't complain. I started riding when I was six—on a pony who was just getting started in the riding business, too—and I've been riding and breaking horses ever since, yet this was my first broken bone.

Copper was foxy today. The wind was in his ears and he was just looking for excuses. It was like a trip back in time, galloping across the newly harvested hayfields on a full-of-the-devil horse. It felt almost the same as it did twenty or more years ago. Only in those days I would have been a lot more careless, almost hoping the horse would go for it, confident I could ride out the storm. Now, things are a bit different. *No, Copper*! Keep your head *up*!

SEPTEMBER 23

It comes around every fall. Cow-moving day. Time to bring the herd home from summer pasture on the north quarter. This year it's on the most beautiful fall day you could ever imagine. The total opposite of last year—as sour a day as could be found in your worst nightmares. Ice-cold rain, mud and slop, in the middle of a run of such evil days. And I with my wrist in a cast. A cast doesn't do well in the pouring rain, so, all things considered, I decided that riding after the cattle that day just wasn't worth it. Instead, I resorted to two bales of hay in the back of the half-ton. It worked, with a little help from some friends. But it didn't work perfectly. The first time I got the whole herd out onto the road a car came along at the strategic moment to spook them all back in again!

But that was then. This is now. By nine o'clock it is warming up and the cows have spread out from their usual fall early-morning vigil at the pasture gate. Some have even crossed to the far side of the soft-bottomed creek. That isn't good. Taking a horse through that bottomless mud is not something I want to try.

Now, cows, the first question is, are you feeling cooperative today or are you going to make this hard for all of us? We're in luck. As I ride into the pasture, heads go up. Bawling starts. The message goes out. "Hey girls, she's finally here. Time to go for winter vacation." Strings of cattle line out toward the gate.

The three calves that have been blissfully grazing in the neighbor's pasture skitter back under the fence and come tearing over to their mothers. Now the bunch of cattle across the creek stare, bawl, finally come jolting, stiff-legged, down the hill, and wade slowly through the creek. Except for two head. The village idiots. They stand on the hill on the other side and gawk, too dim to comprehend what every other critter has already figured out.

The rest of the cattle line up at the gate while those two gawk some more. The others begin to fidget. I begin to fidget. I ride up and down the creek bank, trying to get the idiots' attention, spook them, do anything to get some action—anything except wallow through that muddy crossing. The idiots take two steps. They gawk. Then something spooks the bunch at the gate. Half of them start moving farther back into the pasture. Back toward the thick willow brush. Oh no you don't! Definitely not the willow brush. We've done the willow brush before. Last time that happened, I was riding a young half-broke Angel horse. By the time that she, I and the cows saw the light of day again, she was a well-broke and thoroughly seasoned cowhorse. Chasing cows by sound in willows too high to see over and too thick to ride through is very educational for all concerned.

The movement of the back-turning renegades catches the attention of the idiots. At last they begin to move toward the creek. I ride to cut off the willow-seekers, urging my horse to hurry but mindful of the gopher holes that pepper the ground beneath her. Funny, I could avoid those gopher holes at a dead gallop when I was fifteen!

The rebels turn, the idiots catch up. We all head for the gate. I wave to my accomplice to open the gate. It's a stiff one. For a minute she wrestles with it. Come on, lady, pull!

The gate's open. The cows stream out onto the road in one compact, calm herd. No straggling calf panics and heads back for the boonies. No deranged mama decides to take her calf and play bunch-quitter at the last second. No confused cow decides to run along the inside of the fence instead of going out. This is almost too good to be true!

Once on the road, it's easy. One neighbor catches up in her truck just before our corner. We pass the time of day. She's in no hurry. Now a car is coming from the west, but we're in luck. The last cow sweeps around the corner and onto our sideroad just in time.

Up the long, slow hill. A minute's visit with Jim Haug, my nearest neighbor who has ambled down to stand in his gateway as the herd goes by.

Then, we're home. I stand in the road, holding Angel and counting as the red and white bodies flow in through the gate. As usual, I count wrong. Two counts later it works out right. I am careful not to count again!

I check my watch. An hour and fifteen minutes have passed since I rode away from the barn. Not bad for riding two miles, gathering the cattle and bringing them two miles back.

Either luck or skill rode with us today. I refuse to speculate on which it was.

SEPTEMBER 24

I let the bulls into the same pasture for the first time since June. They might as well get their social status sorted out in their stubborn little brains. Halvor has been hanging around the corral, just itching to get at Chester—who happens to be his father. This is the first year that Halvor has thought himself bull enough to challenge the old man. Just like a teenager who decides he's finally big enough to hang a licking on Pop.

So they got together and pushed each other over a few acres of trees. When I left, they were still pushing, with Missy yelping encouragement like some empty-headed cheerleader. Finally even she got bored and came home, a little hoarse from her efforts.

This evening I went out to see if anyone was still alive. Sure enough, Chester was keeping company with a heifer in heat, no doubt the cause of all this macho competition. Occasionally, Halvor made a tentative move in the heifer's direction but Chester just lowered his head and the lad backed off.

Five hundred pounds and a few years' seniority will outlast youth and athletic ability any day. Good news for the over-the-hill gang. But then again, Chester is going to market this fall . . .

There were three jets in the sky at once today, all heading southwest. To Vancouver, maybe? Tiny silver arrows trailing white chalk lines across a cobalt sky. Beautiful. But, *three*? This country's getting *too* civilized.

SEPTEMBER 25

Another perfect day but the trees are showing a little wear. A few more bare spots. Gray trunks that yesterday were hidden by curtains of gold. The carpet on the ground thickens. The balsam poplars lose their leaves first. A shiftless sort of tree, they're the last to leaf out in the spring, too. What's with this short work year? They must be unionized.

I rode Copper up to the south quarter to see the cattle. Went up by a trail we cleared the deadfall from this summer. The work was worthwhile. It was a beautiful ride, sun-dappled shade and a thousand autumn-forest smells along the way.

Coming home through the fields, Copper thought it would be fun to have just *one* little go at bucking again. I told him firmly, no, and made him run a couple of up-the-hill circles to purify his mind. Then we came on home, peacefully.

SEPTEMBER 26

Fall has gone a little past her prime. The sun was not quite so bright today, although it was still Indian-summer warm. It didn't feel so much like a day to walk or ride. It was a hunkering-down day, a day to stick close to home and prepare the den for winter. So I split wood.

September still is smiling, but now it's kind of a sad smile.

SEPTEMBER 27

The cats come trooping in for breakfast, their little fur-trimmed leather slippers padding busily across the carpet.

We have come to the rustling season—leaves, not cows! Everywhere you step, they crackle underfoot. It's a poor time for sneaking.

When I was a kid, in my Zane Grey phase, I used to try to be like Lew Wetzel, the great Indian scout (Indian killer, too, come to think of it, but my savage child's mind was uninhibited by such trivial details). In Grey's "eastern westerns," Wetzel could move through the great hardwood forests as silently as a ghost. Well, Wetzel, I challenge you to do it here, at this time of year. Even the cats move noisily through the bush.

I tried to pose The Prince for a picture beside the wonderfully colored red osier dogwood bush. Five times I dragged him out of its shady depths. Six times he crawled back in before I could take the picture. All the while, Missy, who exudes a distinct odor of skunk these days, was right there next to my nose, "helping" me.

The butterflies are out today in the hot Indian summer sun, orange and brown velvet ones. Happy. Unaware that, surely, in a few days they will be dead. What does that matter? That will be then. Today the sun is shining. The world is wonderful.

At dusk tonight there was a concert. It began with the bass, a distant great gray owl, singing out his loneliness and lost love. Who? Who? Who?

Then, on percussion, a nearby woodpecker joined in. Three beats on a tree trunk.

A coyote in the west began to add his plaintive notes. Hank Williams? No, maybe Buck Owens.

Sure enough. A coyote in the south joins in, doing a Dwight Yoakam rendition.

Now, the owl again.
Three more taps by the woodpecker.
The coyotes in harmony.
Now *that's* country music.

SEPTEMBER 28

I am drunk on sunshine. I finished school at noon, came home and tossed the groceries, still in their bags, onto the table, then headed for the deck to start absorbing light and heat. The sun is very warm, tanning warm, but not hot enough to be uncomfortable. The sky is blue from horizon to horizon and the breeze rustles noisily through the crisp dry leaves still clinging to the trees. In some directions, the trees are nearly bare while, in others, they are still loaded with gold. With each passing breeze, a golden snow falls to the ground.

Blue jays and magpies, species blessed with singing voices much like mine, fill the woods with the scrawking gabble of their political conventions while, beside me on the deck, the dog snores the rapid, half-panting snores of a dog too hot to be comfortable and too dumb to move.

I lie staring at the sun through closed eyelids, something I remember doing ever since I was a little kid. A kaleidoscope of colors—all the reds, beginning at ruby with eyelids squeezed together, then loosening notch by notch to crimson, scarlet, orange, until, with eyes almost open, the world turns emerald green.

SEPTEMBER 29

Another day of sun—so hot that, while I fixed a broken wire on the high field, sweat ran down my face.

SEPTEMBER 30

The last day of September and the last day of Indian summer—at least this phase of it. But when I woke up—late because it was Saturday—I was surprised. The sun was pouring in. Maybe the forecasts were wrong. I rushed outside without even combing my hair to discover September's parting gift. Brilliant sunshine in the east, reflecting off heavy blue-gray thunderclouds in the west. My favorite kind of light. I rambled around the yard, taking pictures, with The Prince right behind me, enjoying the spectacle.

Half an hour later, the magic was gone, replaced by lowering clouds and a sour wind.

Tonight has become a night of howling wind, complaining around the windows and spitefully snatching at the few remaining leaves. A wind of change.

I walked out into it just before dark, saddened by the end of the warm, lazy fall days but somehow a little excited by the challenge in the wind, awakened from a sleepy season and ready to fight the tough months ahead.

And not that far ahead. The clouds tonight hung heavy-bellied and low. Snow clouds? I wouldn't be surprised. The woods behind the barn were full of complaining cows this afternoon. The horses followed me around the barnyard, making demands. The dog and cats—even the formidably-furred Prince—are in the house this evening, behaving themselves perfectly, not making waves and chancing being exiled from the cosy house. What do the animals know that I don't know?

OCTOBER 3 and 4

It didn't snow last weekend after all. The animals lied. It did get cold, though. Less than 20°F. That's colder than many winter nights.

But today was warm again, during the sunshine hours. I went to renew acquaintances with the beaver dam. There were about forty ducks on it. I could hear their conversation long before I could see them. Ducks are the one creature that make exactly the sound we attribute to them. In fact, to me, a duck sounds exactly like a human trying to quack like a duck!

There is already a thin film of ice on the shady backwaters, and the mud along the edges is frost-hard. It's going to be a *long* winter.

I was thinking about that at the end of September. It will be almost six months before we come around to even equal amounts of light and darkness. This *is* hard country.

On my way to school this morning, I saw a porcupine ambling down the road. Naturally, I slowed down and waited for him to get out of the way. Hours later, as I was coming home, there he was again. Again I waited.

Next morning, I fully expected to find him there again, smeared all over the road by a driver less patient than I, or more inclined to collect road kills the way a gunfighter collects notches on his gun. But I was wrong. No dead porky. Either he was a lucky one, or smart enough to know which drivers to trifle with!

OCTOBER 5

I must have averaged fifty miles per hour on my way to school today. Sounds reasonable enough—except that the average came from doing eighty part way to make up for doing twenty—all the time I watched a big, old cow moose cross almost the entire north quarter at a kind of shambling trot, which she interspersed with periodic stops to gawk in all directions. Didn't anyone ever tell her that open quarter isn't moose country?

OCTOBER 6

It was one of those movie-making mornings. A time when the country looks like it's auditioning for a remake of *Gone with the Wind*.

The sun was rising pure gold in the eastern sky, but between here and the sun, banks of fog rose, too, diffusing the sun's glow into a soft creaminess. The whole world was wrapped in mystery.

Lines of gray-clad gentlemen on hot-blooded horses should have emerged from the fog and paused in the horizon for a moment before riding off into gallant death.

OCTOBER 8

Yesterday I went cow-chasing, gathering up the bunch from the south quarter and bringing them home through the thick brush, down trails known only to cows and designed to fit only cows—not horses with riders on top.

This was an accidental sort of roundup. All summer I had carefully kept at home, separate from the rest, a little bunch of cattle that I was going to sell. When I brought the main herd home from summer pasture, again I carefully set this bunch aside and added to it a couple of heifers I'd been keeping for a neighbor and a steer that is to be butchered this fall. These stayed in the home pasture. The rest went to the south quarter.

I made arrangements with a neighbor to butcher the steer next week. I was *so* organized. All I had to do was slip the steer into the corral. That is, I was *so* organized until one little thing went wrong. Ken Walker, the friend who cuts my hay on shares, started hauling bales from the field this weekend. Between the field and the feed corral there are two gates to be opened. There is nothing more frustrating when you're in a hurry than to have to stop, open the gate, drive through, stop, close the gate, four times on each round trip from the field. Solution? Just leave the gates open. The cows are

nowhere in sight so they must be grazing way over on the far side of the pasture. Just keep an eye out for them and everything will move much faster . . .

I knew that was what Ken was doing. And I knew what was going to happen. How did I know? Because I've tried the same trick a few dozen times myself. Sometimes, you get away with it.

Casually, in passing, I mentioned to Ken that there *were* cows in this pasture. He replied, confidently, that indeed there were and he was watching for them.

Early that evening the phone rang. It was Ken. Confident had turned to apologetic. "About those cows in, no those cows that *used to be in*, the small pasture . . ."

Needless to say, a joyous cow reunion was under way, even as we spoke. So I got a chance to go cowboying. It wasn't so bad. Not if you don't count the four-inch rip in my new jeans, caused by a branch that jumped right out and bit me.

Actually, I saw some territory I hadn't looked at for a while, got my adrenalin up, appreciated the abilities of Angel to chase cows by sound when the brush is too thick to see them—and came home feeling young and daring again. Probably an adequate reward for a little extra work.

I walked in the last of the daylight tonight. The sky was still blue but it had lost its light and was fading softly to gray. The woods were bright, though, with a rustling carpet of still-golden leaves.

Usually it's a little lonely in the woods at dusk, but not tonight. The cows were there, a big, fat, contented old girl grazing behind every tree. Sometimes I wonder why I bother with cows. Tonight I know why. I'd miss them so much if they weren't there.

There was another animal out this evening. Up ahead, I saw Missy doing her forward and back jumping routine—the one she uses when she plays war games with The Prince. But this was no Prince, it was a porky sitting there bunched up against a fallen tree!

"Missy! *No!*" I yelled, and, wonder of wonders, she listened. Is it because she has finally grown up, or because she already learned about porcupines with a nose full of quills last spring?

Anyway, we step back and study the porky with discretion. He's just a little fellow, a ball of coarse hair and quills with the harmless face of a nearsighted rabbit. We find we have no quarrel with each other. Missy and I head for home, leaving the night woods to the other animals.

This time of year is for the birds. The trees and skies are full of them. A raven passes overhead with wings that move with the sound of rustling silk. If he'd keep his mouth shut and not let out his graceless squawk he could be a bird of considerable elegance. (An observation I would sometimes do well to consider in my own case!)

As Missy and I walk through the spruce woods a ruffed grouse lifts sudden and spooky almost from under my feet. Her heavy wingbeats send the dry leaves whirling.

Blue jays sail about the yard, ever watchful for the moment when the dog's unfinished food is left unguarded, then swooping down to steal a tidbit and soar away like happy bandits.

A whisky jack makes a temporary landing on the railing of the deck, pauses to sort out a beakful of struggling bug, then flies off again.

The spruce trees are alive with chickadees, twinkling in and out of the branches like strings of tiny Christmas tree lights.

Nuthatches scurry up and down tree trunks, forgetting to act like birds at all. Maybe they're an error of nature—squirrels accidentally placed in birds' bodies.

As daylight fades I hear a knocking, high up in a half-dead poplar. I look up. There he is, the industrious woodpecker, alternately hammering and squeaking excitedly as he digs out dinner.

With the dying of the light comes the requiem for the day. Deep in the darkening woods a solitary owl calls out. Hoo, Hoo, Hoo-Hoo.

Night has fallen.

October 10

The first snow of the year came unexpectedly at midday, swept in on a mighty wind that blew my road gate shut and knocked over a big tree down by the creek. First came the clouds, then rain, then little hail pellets, then sheets of snow. An hour later it was all over. A skim of snow lay across the ground and melted on the trees to fall in crystal teardrops.

By evening, the storm clouds had scattered and lay heaped along the horizons, turning, at sunset, into huge purple and pink mountains. Violent, stormy days always bring the most exciting sunsets. Is that also true of life, I wonder.

October 11

Chester went to market today. For a rancher, I've got it all backward: exchanging a living animal for a cheque always fills me with a sense of guilt and betrayal. From the time the truck takes them away until I'm sure they're dead, I'm miserable, thinking about the fear and confusion they must be going through.

So, what am I doing in the cattle business? Well, I'm not a vegetarian so, as long as I can go on enjoying a Big Mac, it's no worse a sin to provide the beef that goes into it. And let's face it, the world will never see great herds of cattle roaming free like antelope on the Serengeti. Being raised for beef is the only role most cattle can play in this society. And, fortunately for them, cattle are not born with the brains to worry about their future. As long as they have lots to eat, good water to drink, warm bedding in the cold of winter and some companionship of their own kind, bovines are blissfully happy. How many of us ever reach that state of contentment?

Tonight, I sat down by the fire, for only a minute, I thought. But, all of a sudden, The Prince launched himself, smiling, into my lap, and lay there, motor humming and all four paws in the air. Naturally, getting up was now out of the question. Kidnapped by a lapcat for a catnap!

OCTOBER 12

A day of opposites. Sunshine so warm I wonder why I have my jacket on. Then, a whistle of wind and a cloud comes scudding in, spitting cold and spiteful rain. We are past autumn's best of times but, still, fragments of beauty hang on. Here and there a poplar tree still blazes yellow, a torch to ward off the gloom of approaching winter. Other poplars stand nearly naked, except for a topknot of gold. These are the candles, their tops a glowing flame to light our way.

The steer was butchered today. Did I feel guilty again? Not really. He was one of the lucky ones who "died in his own bed," almost. One well-placed bullet in the head by my neighbor, Jim, who is an excellent butcher. Aside from getting irritable about being corralled, the steer was scarcely inconvenienced by his own death. And fortunately, this steer, like most I've kept for butchering, had grown into an ugly, overbearing and thoroughly obnoxious animal, whose demise I had anticipated almost eagerly at times.

It did make me stop and think, though, when I looked at the sides of beef hanging cooling in the shed overnight. It was nice-looking meat. But just that, meat. A few short hours ago, it was a living, feeling animal, with a personality (however obnoxious) of its own.

What a strange thing the spark of life is. Where does that mysterious force in living things go when they are dead? What is the essential difference between being alive and being dead? The question goes far beyond my butchered steer, all the way to medical-ethics committees who must decide about life-support systems, mercy killing and organ transplants from brain-dead donors. I hope the answers come more easily to them than to me, but never too easily.

OCTOBER 14

Birds again! Flights of elegant magpies in black and white formal attire, sailing through the last grove of golden trees. Whisky jacks, too, the softest-looking of all the birds. Even their pearl-gray color is soft.

A mile or two down the road is the little flock of Hungarian partridges. Such meek, unassuming little birds, scuttling along, heads down, like nuns on their way to vespers. And right in the backyard, the ruffed grouse. Not nearly so meek. Beautifully patterned feathers on display as he stands tall and stretches his neck to look around.

OCTOBER 16

If fall is a kind of crossbred season—half summer, half winter—then today is a true fall day. The sun is warm and brilliant, shining in a clear blue sky. A sun to remember summer by. But wind is another story. Straight off an iceberg! The midwinter wind would be hard-pressed to blow much colder. The sun and wind today remind me of the story in an old reader about the competition the sun and wind held to make a traveller take off his cloak. The wind tried to blow it off but failed. The sun simply warmed him up until he took it off willingly. I wish the sun would win today's competition!

But despite the wind, it is a day well worth keeping. Only a few straggling yellow leaves remain but the lawn is still as green as summer. The low-angled October sun seems to feel duty-bound to atone for the lack of color in the trees by back-lighting each trunk and twig with a silver glow. Light-encircled birds fly back and forth to the feeder to get the fat I've just put out for them (with hopes that it's now too late in the season for a bear to come and get it, as happened one year). An adventurous squirrel, haloed in light as though each hair were tipped with frost, explores the very end of a shining spruce bough.

The air has a crystal sharpness, so clean it seems to carry the tang of fresh-washed laundry. An occasional bluish drift of woodsmoke from the chimney seems only to emphasize the air's freshness, adding its own aroma to the perfume that is fall. There is something deeply reassuring about a little woodsmoke at this time of year. Yes, you can go outside and enjoy the challenge of the elements. But just inside is a big, black stove, a warm chair and hot coffee.

OCTOBER 18

Last week I had a momentary attack of efficiency and decided to put away the deck chairs before they ended up outside all winter, as has been known to happen. I did put most of them away but some incurable streak of optimism made me leave just a couple out. And sure enough, here I am on the deck again, revelling in hot sunshine and a delicate chinook breeze.

It's so quiet today. Not even much wildlife about. The animals are probably all asleep in the sun, like the Timothy cat, who is being a disgusting couch potato, sleeping inside on the sun-drenched carpet. One woodpecker did stop by, landing on the railing and reconnoitering before deciding on a better spot for lunch. Oh, I spoke about peace and quiet too soon. Missy just discovered me lying here in the lounge chair and very nearly smothered me with kisses before I could escape.

I've been splitting wood again, trying to get the last of my decrepit old woodpile split and stacked so I can bring in some new blocks. I love everything about wood: the scouting walks to discover what new windfall nature has provided, the cutting of the dead and fallen trees so the pasture can grow better, the hauling, the splitting, the carrying, the smell of woodsmoke at dusk, the penetrating woodstove warmth, even the carrying out of ashes and seeing how matter really can be transformed into energy, big armloads of wood gone and only a little box of talcum-fine ash left behind.

OCTOBER 19

A fall chinook day. It dawned warm and soft with a pearly sky, a big bank of purple, pink and gold clouds in the north and mountains standing out like cardboard cutouts. By midday, the sky was blazing blue in the east and blazing blue in the west with a heavy bank of chinook cloud overhead. There is something magical about the chinook arch, which brings a special light and a special quality to the day.

Here, wrapped in the chinook's warm and friendly arms, it is hard to believe that last night the earth turned mean in California, terrorizing San Francisco with its worst earthquake in more than eighty years. I can't imagine living in a place where the promise of "the big one" hangs heavy in the air.

Earthquakes, like many other natural disasters, are magnified by man's insistence on clustering himself in ever-larger megalopolises. An earthquake in the country would be so much less terrifying. No double-decker highways to trap cars in their jaws. No tall buildings crumbling onto hapless passers-by. Unless a person was unlucky enough to be swallowed up by a crack in the earth itself or zapped by a falling tree, the danger here would be slight.

So what if fallen trees blocked the road? Stay home. Eat the meat from the freezer and the vegetables from the cold room. Read a good book. Electricity out? Propane line damaged? Shut it all off. Light the kerosene lamps and fill the stoves with all that wood I'm so obsessed with splitting. And eat *lots* of meat. I forgot what would happen to the stuff in the freezer when the power went out.

OCTOBER 21

Things were slow getting started this Saturday morning. I got up by daylight but that seemed to be my only achievement. The Tim cat hung around underfoot, waiting to be fed. The dog whined outside, begging me to come out and play. The big black monster-stove proved conclusively, as I lit and relit its fire five times, that there is no shred of truth in the old adage that where there's smoke there's fire.

Then the sun came in, lighting up the big south windows, which leered at me like street urchins with filthy faces. Ashamed, I immediately got out the Windex and attacked them. But I might as well have listened to the dog and gone for a walk instead. As usually happens with my window washing, the dirt is not gone, only redistributed. Now the window grins evilly at me through its streaks. If I attack the inside, the streaks move to the outside. I rush outside and they appear inside. Guess I'll just have to close the drapes.

It turned into a choring kind of day. A walk up to check the cattle found them out of salt so I made a trip to the Bergen store for salt and a few groceries. I took the salt up to the field and stopped on the way back to saw up a big poplar that fell on the fence in last week's windstorm. Then the job of splicing and tightening the wires. I never get it right, but maybe it *looks* fixed enough to fool some of the cows some of the time.

OCTOBER 22

A sunny Sunday morning. I am being lazy, dawdling over breakfast after I get the animals fed and out. Obviously I have dawdled too long. The Prince is now lying on the outside windowsill, beside the table, dirtying the window and letting me know he wants *in*. Morris is climbing the door—he's an absolutely ancient cat; wouldn't you think he'd be too stiff for such nonsense? And Missy is renovating her house. She does this regularly, like a bored housewife rearranging the furniture. She removes her blankets and races around the yard with them like a football player going for a touchdown, and finally leaves them draped artistically across the lawn for me to pick up.

October 23

One of those heavy chinook days. Brooding cloud most of the day, making it seem cold when really the temperature was quite warm. Twilight seemed to fall in midafternoon. And then, just before slipping over the horizon, the sun found the narrow chinook arch of clear sky and, for a few minutes, managed to paint a golden rim along the tops of the trees in the east and then bathe the land in a warm gold-rose glow as it set.

October 24

It was raining lightly this morning, and *dark*. I could hardly find my way out the door at eight o'clock. But, the rain stopped and the morning turned soft, a word I think the Irish use to describe this mild, misty kind of weather.

As I drove to school under a sky just lightening to the first gray of dawn, an owl perched damply in a tree by the road, probably trying to decide if it was day or night.

Minutes later, the sun rose, in cloud too thick to let it shine, but still casting a warm neon-pink glow above the eastern horizon.

This afternoon, a cattle buyer came to list the calves for computer sale. My cattle behave just like children. When it's just family, they're totally tame and well-behaved, but let me bring guests to show them off to, and the whole herd hightails it to the brush like stampeded buffalo.

October 25

A cloudy day again. At sunrise, a chinook arch spread all the way around three sides of the sky, leaving only the eastern horizon in cloud that turned to pink cotton candy as the sunrise touched it.

October 26

A warm day for late October. Warm enough to sit on the deck—with a jacket on. It was perfectly still out there. Then one sound:

the sharp, clear tapping of a woodpecker on a tree down by the creek.

OCTOBER 27

A gray day: gray skies, gray trees, a gray feeling.

But trust Missy to contribute a little light entertainment. She comes trotting into the yard, carrying a disgusting old bone she has disinterred from her secret burying ground. A morsel must have dropped off because a magpie suddenly swoops down behind her, after something on the ground. Missy spots him, swings around and charges, her mouth so full of bone that she'd have to grab the bird in her bare paws if she ever caught up to him.

Magpie nonchalantly flutters up to a low branch. Vindicated, dog goes on her way. Magpie swoops down again. Dog tears back in a terrible flap, bone still gripped in her teeth. Magpie escapes once more. Dog goes on her way. Magpie returns. The whole scenario replays half a dozen times. At last, in desperation, dog drops her bone to do serious battle. Magpie still escapes.

The only less dignified performance I've seen by a dog was when Stormy, the huge old German shepherd, would take exception to an occasional chickadee that had the audacity to lunch on her abandoned bones. When over a hundred pounds of shepherd is in full pursuit of a couple of ounces of bird it's hard to cheer for the underdog!

Speaking of chickadees, the first one showed up for a handout at the windowsill feeder today. Is this, then, the official first day of winter for this country?

Just at dusk there's a whole convention of birds. I hear the sound of geese overhead. Unlike the ducks, who sound so much like ducks that I think they're faking, geese do not sound at all like geese. Whatever that wild haunting cry may be, it does not say *honk* to me. It is a wonderful sound, though, eerie and skin-prickling. In fall it is unbearably sad, filled with the despair of death and winter. In April it is hope and spring.

As I look up I spot five geese flying southwest. Geese mate for life. Is there a tragedy in this odd number or is one of them just a rebel single like me? I also see a great gray owl perched in a spruce nearby and being scolded by two blue jays and a whisky jack. On the lane beneath the tree, stalking along big-tailed and stiff-legged, is His Excellency, The Prince. Has he seen the owl? Has the owl seen The Prince? Who is planning on eating who? (No pun intended.) The two of them, though eons apart biologically, could be cousins with their serious round faces, huge accusing eyes, and big soft ball-of-fluff bodies.

While I gaze, fascinated, at this multifaceted scene there is a scrabbling noise and a new player hits the field. It's Missy, charging in carrying her current favorite toy, a stiff old chunk of carpet, shaking it vigorously in a vain attempt to kill it, and wanting desperately to join the party down here.

All this commotion is too much for a quiet, scholarly bird. For an instant, the owl's eyes seem to grow rounder still. Then, on silent wings, he's gone.

Missy sets her carpet down, grins and tries to figure out what was so interesting in the first place. The Prince arches his back, warning her about the consequences of any foolish doggy actions. Missy settles for another session of carpet killing. I scoop The Prince up onto my shoulder. We all go home.

OCTOBER 28

Dire promises of snow in the forecast last night. We didn't get any, but Banff did. The mountains are white castles this morning. Today began gray but by early afternoon there was bright sun and a clear blue sky. Just cold enough for a good brisk work day.

A day of yard jobs and wood jobs. As I split wood a squirrel scolds from a branch just above my head. Then, he's gone, scampering off along his private sky-tram, from branch-tip to branch-tip all across the north slope of the yard. Then he's up onto the double-coated wire that brings power across from the barnyard, and a quick skitter to the next convenient tree. Nice way to travel, if you've got the balance for it.

For most of the evening, the dog and cats are sound asleep in the house. Nothing makes a room cosier than four fur rugs—complete with original contents—draped tastefully about the floor and furniture.

Then, about the time that *I'm* thinking of sleep, they all wake up. Missy goes out to begin her regular evening bark. At what, I'm not sure. Probably coyotes. I don't think she scares them much, but what she lacks in ferocity she makes up in sheer persistence. This concert can go on for an hour or two.

Now, each of the cats selects a way to be difficult. Morris, so old he must be senile, takes a sudden kittenish spell and chases a Ping-Pong ball through the house. Not to be outdone, The Wicked Prince chases *Morris.* Timothy, the overweight, three-legged, elder statesman, chooses this exact moment, even as I try to write, to hurtle into my lap like an upholstered cannonball, purring so loud I can't concentrate.

OCTOBER 29

The first day off daylight saving time. I awake about twenty-to-eight into the first bright sunlight. A pleasant change from bumbling around in the early-morning dark but I know I'll hate it this afternoon when darkness creeps in far too early.

I put the bacon and coffee to simmering, and Missy and I head out for a ten-minute walk. At the first tiny creek she stops for her morning drink. But the water isn't wet any more! Puzzled, she gives it an experimental scratch. The ice holds. She gives a dog shrug and philosophically trots on. The big creek will be open. It is.

There's a blue jay having a fit outside my kitchen window. There are sunflower seeds on the outside windowsill and he wants them. No, it's worse—he lusts for them! But I am in full view at the table just inside. The bird is in a quandary. Which is stronger, his desire for the seeds or his fear of the ogre? He dithers. A brief landing on the windowsill. No, his nerves can't stand the strain of looking at me. He's gone again. Onto the lilac bush to sit, shimmering iridescent blues from his twitching feathers. He squawks in frustration. He flies up to the roof, peers over the edge. I am still here. Will I never leave?

The blue jay is one of our most beautiful birds but winning friends and influencing people are not a part of his repertoire.

Marilyn and Ken Walker have been close friends of mine since high school, and are my ever-available "emergency response team" through an endless array of country crises. No crisis today, but they come from their place on the other side of Sundre for a late-season wiener roast this afternoon. The campsite at the bottom of the yard is deep in crunchy leaves and the air is chill enough to make the fire feel really good. It's the kind of day when being out around a fire seems bold and adventurous, especially when you're just a hundred yards from a warm house with a big cheerful black stove inside.

As we sit around the fire, there is a sudden rustle and crackle and we look up, startled by the sight of a four-legged black thunderbolt barrelling down the hill, half out-of-control and barely managing to brake to a skidding stop at the edge of the fire-pit. It's only Missy, making an entrance as she returns from some doggy mission. It must have suddenly occurred to her that we might be eating something in her absence so haste was of the essence. A split-second miscalculation on her part and "hot dog" would have taken on a whole new meaning.

OCTOBER 30

This time the storm warnings didn't lie. The ground is white tonight and fitful squalls send more feathers floating down. It came on suddenly, just after noon. When I came home at twelve it was warm so I left the doors open to let the sunshine in while I buried myself in the basement, cleaning the freezer. (I have such an exciting life!)

An hour later, I surfaced again, looked out, blinked and looked again. The first squall, miniature hail pellets, had already come and gone, a scattering of white left behind on the ground. Minutes later, the snow struck. In a wet blizzard, I walked across the barnyard to feed the horses. I saw a flash of light and concluded I was going crazy, until I heard the crash of thunder. That little display out of its system, the weather settled down, forgot summer flashbacks, and got on with the snowing.

The chimney cleaner came this afternoon—and not a moment too soon. Tonight, the fires blaze brightly and the fur people and I cocoon.

OCTOBER 31

Winter! An inch or more of snow and the temperature is sticking at a few degrees below freezing. (Ever since metric came in I hesitate to talk in specific degrees due to my perpetual confusion—not to mention irritation.)

I wish I could be one of those perky little people who witter endlessly about the joys of snow and cold and all that wonderful stuff. But I can't. Winter is not my season. To me it means putting on boots for a quick dash to start the car or burn the garbage—or most anything else, for that matter. It means extra chores just to keep the world unfrozen. And it means frosty windows on vehicles. Which brings me to my first act of this winter's comedy.

Before school, I decided it was a day to drive my little 4 X 4 truck instead of the "tractionless toy" Firebird Trans Am I drive in good weather. Unfortunately, the truck was parked in the far corner of the yard, ensconced in ice and snow. Well, I'd just slip on my boots and drive it up to the door so I could jump in with just my shoes to go to town. That was a wonderful idea, until, in my hurry to back the truck out of its parking spot, without stopping to clear the back window, I backed right smack into a tree. No major damage, thanks to a big back bumper. The tree has decided not to press charges.

By evening, which now is any time after about four-thirty, my mood had improved enough to take a walk through a snowy, unpastured field. A dozen varieties of interesting dry weeds stood out in contrast to the bed of snow beneath them. I even picked a "bouquet," something I rarely do in summer.

November 1

The weather is improving. A chinook is on its way. When I walked at dawn there was a friendly sky of peach and gray-turning-blue.

November 2

When I drove out onto the road at daylight a huge bull elk was standing just 200 yards away, in the middle of the road. I drove toward him, trying to remind him that this *was* hunting season. He caught on and made the right decision. He trotted off on *my* side of the road—where the NO HUNTING signs are on the fence.

I was away all day on a school field trip and came home in the early dark, tired of cities and crowds, and very tired of school buses. And a little more frustrated by the fact I'd left my keys locked inside the truck when I got on the bus!

A walk out into the star-studded silence after supper put the world back in its proper perspective.

November 3

A beautiful, warm, chinook morning. The dog and I walked into a rose-pink sunrise that filled the whole eastern sky and reflected on the land below. Ice on the road, dry grass, even tree trunks, took on a warm, rosy glow. In the northeast, the sky was stratified, layer upon layer of flat clouds, turning thin air into sedimentary rock. Gradually, as we walked home, the pink faded and changed to a clear light orange, orange ice cream à la cloud.

November 4

I woke to the end of an overnight rain. Puddles everywhere and the air soft and moist. The remnants of the snow are almost washed away. It's a west coast morning. This is how it looked in Victoria last spring, everything newly washed and still damp. Out of character for Alberta in November, but I'll take it over the cold any day.

November 5

A mostly sunny day, interrupted by occasional clouds spitting little fits of rain.

I brought the cattle home from the south field in the late afternoon. Coming out of the field, the low sun sends our immensely tall, ghostly shadows ahead of us. Who is this gaunt, wavering rider on a stilt-legged horse, driving spectral cattle into the dusky woods? Could this be the ghost herd from the sky?

Once home, I put the horse away and feed the cattle some hay. As the herd gathers around I get an uneasy feeling. The bunch looks too small. I count. Fifteen head are missing. I jump in the truck and drive around the road to the west quarter. Sure enough, the truants had left the main herd and crossed the creek into the north fields.

Riding in the setting sun was good romantic stuff, but now it's almost dusk and I need these cows at home. So I crank up the truck radio, drum my fingers on the roof and stampede them? Not likely. As I said earlier, my cows only go loco for company. Now, they stand chewing their cuds and gawking at me in mild amazement.

The lady's really lost it this time, girls. Oh well, humor her. With the cow equivalent of a shrug, they file out toward home, to the accompaniment of a golden oldie station playing the Beatles at rock concert volume. Sorry to tell you this, Boys from Liverpool, but you're over the hill. Not a single cow screamed or fainted.

As we leave the field, the only light is the gray sky. Against it, tree-covered hills stand like faraway crew-cut heads.

In the almost-dark woods, cows slip like shadows through the trees. Two trot purposefully past the truck. Whoa! Those two aren't cows, they're moose. A cow and her half-grown calf. At least these two have escaped the rotten hunters so far. I wish them well and head for the welcoming light and warmth of the house.

NOVEMBER 7

The lilac bush was full of chickadees today. Winter is *their* season! There is a crackling of twigs high above me. I look up. A big fat grouse, incongruously tiptoeing in the high poplar branches.

NOVEMBER 8

Took a day off school today to send the calves away to a feedlot to be fattened. They were already sold, by computer, last week. I was quite proud of them, a nice-looking bunch, but again, the thought of a cheque wasn't enough to completely erase my guilty conscience. It still seems a little wrong, somehow, for one species to live off of the misfortune of another. But of course that's the way it was meant to be. Otherwise, what would happen to all the beautiful carnivores of the world who were born to kill in order to eat? And with the cattle, it's not a one-way deal. These cows would never survive an Alberta winter without a human making sure the hay was put up in the summer and doled it out to them when it's forty below.

Still, it's a sad time, splitting families and taking away the calves that have been the cows' reason for living for the past eight months. But in about three days, the cows will begin to forget their kidnapped babies. After all, they are already about six months' pregnant again. If I didn't wean these calves the cows would do it themselves soon. A winter vacation from motherhood is not entirely unwelcome.

As for the calves, tonight they're in a feedlot way down in Medicine Hat country. It will seem strange. They will miss the trees—those wonderful, aromatic scratching posts—but they'll find that there is food. Grain! They'd never known that such a wonderful taste existed. And water. And bedding to sleep on. They'll get along. Tonight they'll cry for their mamas. By next week their main concern will be who's first to the feed trough!

NOVEMBER 9

I take a five-minute walk this morning and am rewarded by the whir of heavy wings on the hillside just below the house. Good news. At least one ruffed grouse is living in the yard this fall.

I cross the bridge and look across to the corral. The replacement heifer calves I've shut up to wean are settling down, happily eating greenfeed. Then I hear a tapping and glance up at the tall dead snag in the big corral. There, high up, busily excavating for ants, is the huge and magnificent pileated woodpecker. Hopefully, he's planning to winter here with us.

This afternoon Ken delivers the new bull I've bought from him to replace Chester. Big, white-and-palomino-spotted Scruffy. Much to Halvor's dismay, his brief reign as top bull is ended. He's number-two son again. But he harasses Scruffy back and forth through the woods for a few hours, trying to prove that it isn't true.

NOVEMBER 10

Whoa! What's going on here? We have *snow* all over the place! It started out with a light sprinkling of small flakes this morning, nothing but a little moisture, really.

Then, just before noon—and just before I had to start out for Calgary—it suddenly got serious, snowing so hard that I almost chickened out on the trip. But I went. At the south corner, on a fencepost, sat a magnificent great gray owl, staring at me disapprovingly over his white moustache, like an elderly English gentleman spotting a woman in his club.

Obviously the owl wasn't intimidated by a little snow, so I took heart and forged on. As I suspected, the farther east I went, the less snow there was. Highway 2 was bare and wet, and very messy.

I had an excellent author visit with the kids at Dr. Egbert School and then set off for home again. The snow grew heavier as I came west. I was glad to be driving the 4 X 4 as I churned through the last few miles of snow and ice.

Home looked wonderful!

NOVEMBER 11

I woke up around five, thanks to The Prince's early-rising habits, and was struck by the absolute silence. The world was muffled and softened with snow. Just two nights ago I'd been awakened by a howling wind that was threatening to bring the huge spruces by the creek crashing through my roof. Now, not a breath.

I got up a bit before daylight and walked out early into the white world. Yes, it was very beautiful. Almost beautiful enough to soften the heart of a confirmed winter-hater. Not quite enough, though, since I couldn't escape the thought of what this was doing to my winter-feeding plans, which included pasturing the cows on second-growth in the hayfields until the end of December. Five or six inches of snow could rearrange things considerably.

Still, I can't resist taking out the camera to finish off the last three frames on my autumn film. I snap three shots. Still, the advancer turns freely. I should be out of film. I shoot again. And again. It turns out that the film was never properly caught on the sprockets. I have now taken twenty-seven pictures on the first frame! So much for my wonderful close-ups of the pileated woodpecker last month. Oh well, I guess that means that I have a whole film to fill with snow pictures.

While I'm out poking around in the field I hear a sound far above. I look up. A long, ragged line of geese is plowing purposefully southeast across a heavy sky. I count, surprised at how hard it is to keep up with the moving line. There are ninety-five of them. They disappear into the distance, still calling back ever-fainter farewells to the north.

Back in the house, I look out at more plebian birds, the ever-present blue jays. One sits on the porch railing, reconnoitering for unguarded dog food. There is none today. He ruffles his crest and scowls. For one fleeting second, his face is exactly that of an irritated Donald Duck. I realize now how carefully the cartoonist has studied real birds.

It's Remembrance Day and, fittingly enough, the day that the Berlin Wall is coming apart. Ironic, all of it. So many people have died, fighting enemies who, short years later, become allies. People die in a hail of bullets, making desperate attempts to cross a wall that now, mainly for political reasons, can be dismantled. The world created by Orwell in *1984* is more truth than fiction.

There is no understanding humanity. I'll stick with the animals—and, of course, a few good friends. Like the ones who spent the evening with me by the fire, digesting a supper of roast beef, mashed potatoes and peas, all grown right here. No preservatives, no additives, just good, old-fashioned calories.

November 12

The whole world is a Christmas card today as channels of blue sky between the snow clouds gradually widen into lakes, seas and, finally, oceans dotted with little cloud islands. I walk up to check the cows in the field. They are grazing happily in the soft new snow, coming up with big mouthfuls of green alfalfa. Snow or no snow they'll manage for a while.

I hear geese again. Another straggling, faintly V-shaped line. This time I count fifty-three. Where will they be tonight? What will they see?

November 13

I walk into a beautiful blue and white early morning. A full moon, turned white in daylight, still floats in the blue morning sky.

November 14

A real smorgasbord kind of a day. All kinds of weather paraded past for sampling. Warm and sparkling with sun for a short while. The mountains gradually drift out of focus and fade into a whitish blur. Then, with a rising wind, a regular blizzard howls in, sending snow whirling and drifting. In an hour it subsides and the sun shines between passing squalls. Then, no more snow, just a sea of cold winter air settling in. This is the real thing, it says. You might as well stop kidding yourself and get out the winter clothes. I only half listen, conceding at last to lined winter gloves. But the gloves I can find are the ones I wore out last winter. Gloves, even lined gloves, with holes in every finger are not particularly cosy. The cause of my problem is not poverty, only stupidity. Halfway through the winter I'll remember to pick up a new pair.

I decide to break down and give the cows a bale. They're not desperate yet, with all that second-growth alfalfa still sticking through the snow, but it's a nasty day . . .

I pick up a bale in the loader's jaws and set off with it up the woods trail, hurrying to get this fifteen-minute job out of the way. But all of a sudden, I'm *not* hurrying! I'm slowing down. Worse yet, I have stopped. I hit the clutch and stare incredulously at my right front tire, almost out of sight in snow and oozing mud, and realize, to my amazement, that the ground isn't frozen. The rain before the snow has turned a soft spot into a bog. I'm not going to drive out of this one. With thoughts best not committed to paper, I trudge home, abandoning the whole mess to a bunch of indignant cows who are hollering bloody murder at me for not getting on with feeding them.

Apologetically (getting stuck is so humiliating!), I call my uncle, who lives two miles down the road. Yes, he'll bring his tractor and haul me out. I hang up, grateful for the thousandth time for good friends and neighbors who are always there when you need them.

He's here in half an hour and in another fifteen minutes my tractor is back on "dry land." I go on feeding, with another bale. I've had to abandon the first one in the mud. A rescue attempt was not worth the risk of getting stuck again! I end up using two bales (enough for about eighty head) for the ten cattle who stuck around and waited. The other thirty-five got disgusted with the wait, said to heck with the whole thing and went back to the field to graze. Obviously, they aren't on their last legs from starvation after all.

I'm cold and tired, and my fifteen-minute job is now done. It took just under two hours. Just one more incident in the continuing saga of why I hate winter.

November 15

Halfway through November. I would like to remind Mother Nature that we are still well within the prescribed limits of fall. *Fall*, I said, as in autumn. So why are we having winter? Why are there several inches of snow? Why did the temperature drop perilously close to zero last night?

Grudgingly, I admit that it was a breathtakingly beautiful morning. (Or maybe my breath was not taken, but frozen!) A pink sky spread its glow over white-washed mountains and fields of snow newly sculpted by yesterday's wind.

NOVEMBER 16

Ah, Alberta *does* have a heart. Chinook! Temperatures above freezing and the sun rising gold through a mass of purple cloud, spilling light as though heaven itself had sprung a leak and its glory was escaping.

NOVEMBER 17

Still chinooky but one of those heavy, cloudy chinook days when it's all you can do to hold the sky up off your shoulders. I make another author visit to a Calgary school.

Calgary crouches dirty-faced and sullen in a cloud of smog, as often happens when a chinook creates an inversion that won't let the dirty air rise. As cities go, Calgary can be such a beautiful city, but she doesn't wear chinooks well. She does still wear her jewels, though, a tiara of the Rockies arcing around her from the southwest, so close it feels like you can reach out and touch them, yet remote and cold as only stone—and some people—can be. Monuments in blue and white, so beautiful it almost hurts to look at them for too long.

NOVEMBER 18

Another heavy, cloudy day. The cows got through the fence into Ken's bale stack for the second time. I had to rush over to the west end and chase them out before heading into Olds to autograph books for a couple of hours.

By afternoon, the chinook was reaching its peak. One gust of wind was so warm I found myself looking around for a fire.

NOVEMBER 19

The chinook howled last night. I awoke at about midnight—actually The Prince woke me, deciding it was going to be a night to prowl.

When I looked out, I couldn't help but agree with him. It was warm and wild out there. A moonlit sky, more blue than black, studded with stars and swept by racing clouds, stood above the blue-gray snow. Huge old spruce trees swayed up and down, one-two, one-two, like matrons at an aerobics class.

Yes, Prince, it's that kind of a night. If I was a young cat, I'd want to go out and howl a little, too.

In the morning, under brilliant sunshine and clear blue skies, I walk up to the field to see the cows. The blanket of snow is moth-eaten by the chinook to a dingy patchwork and the cows graze angelically, far from yesterday's molested bale yard. "Who, us?" they say. "Get in the bales? We're not that kind of girls!"

And they probably won't be—until the next snow. This spring-like morning, that seems a long way off. Only one thing causes me to doubt a little. The wind, that slight, gentle breeze on my face, seems to have turned around to the north . . .

I should have known. By early afternoon, it's snowing, a fine, damp little snow that's almost a mist. I rush around getting in a good supply of dry wood. Soon it's snowing in earnest, undoing all the work of my lovely chinook!

NOVEMBER 21

Yesterday was snow-showery. Another two or three inches accumulated. It turned sunny again this afternoon and cold tonight. It will probably hit perilously close to 0°F tonight.

It was not a day for appreciating the simple pastoral joys of having cattle. When I got home from school at two-thirty, I found the notorious Apron cow dining on a bale of green feed in the hay corral. Further investigation showed that the bar gate had been rubbed down and the bulls were both standing in the gateway munching on a bale. The only good thing was that the big lugs effectively plugged the opening, keeping the rest of the bunch outside!

I sorted that mess out and proceeded to the field to give the ingrates a legal bale of hay from the feed corral up there. And what do I find but that fence broken, too, and a cow and calf inside helping themselves.

I spent the rest of the afternoon fixing fence. I do not love cows tonight.

November 22

As pretty a winter day as ever comes along. Orange ice-cream sunrise this morning and a day turned sparkling blue and white by noon. Trees frosted, every twig outlined in white.

But, by no means a warm day. No melting on the roads, which are glassy and treacherous. The trip to town takes half again as long as it should.

But, the cows stayed out of the bales. That rates it as a good day.

November 23

As a chinook comes in again, I drive to school under a sky almost too beautiful to take in. Warm rose and that special blue that comes only with chinook sunrises. Along the road, a little herd of horses stands against the sunrise sky, a picture too wonderful for mere reality. Bring on the movie cameras again!

November 24

Colder again. The kind of day for brisk winter chores. Sawed some wood, and my friend Marilyn helped me load and unload it.

November 25

A day without sunshine. Meteorologically, that is. A range of weather from dull sky to a few periods of fairly heavy snow. Emotionally speaking, it wasn't as depressing as some dark, heavy days. Maybe I was too busy to be depressed. I got some more wood and then took a long walk to check on the cows' behavior, which was quite good, for a change. I saw the pileated woodpecker. Yesterday both the downy and the hairy woodpecker were at the bag of fat by the window. The woodpecker clan is quite complete.

I spent the evening with Marilyn and Ken, eating a comforting winter supper of potato soup and hot lemon pudding, and then sharing a couple of hours by the fire with conversation, music, warmth and the charm of *their* three spoiled cats.

November 26

A day *full* of sunshine. What a difference it makes. After my morning walk I came in convinced it must be almost thawing out there. But when I checked the temperature it was actually colder than yesterday.

As Missy and I walked through the woods, a raven flew low across the trail ahead of us. In a flash, Missy was in hot pursuit. Poor dog, she still hasn't figured out that she really can't fly!

Later, after feeding the cows, we walked up to check the horses, rustling on the south hayfields for the winter. They were fine, fat as seals. But I did have a panic-stricken moment when I saw four of them right together and no sign of Angel. With hunting season on, I had visions of my palomino in brown-wrapped packages in some dim-witted hunter's freezer—"You know, Ethel, that was the lightest-colored deer I ever did see . . ."

After losing almost-thirty-year-old Reb last spring (natural causes, I think; it was August when we came upon his skeleton in the deep woods on the west quarter after days of fruitless searching in April) I'm a little paranoid about missing horses.

However, this time there's a happy ending. Angel is just over a little hill, grazing placidly.

NOVEMBER 30

For the first time in a too-busy week, I had a chance to walk through the woods today. It's a perfect chinook day, just at the melting point, the air soft and warm with sunshine from a bright blue sky. The only sounds in the woods were the occasional quarrelsome squawks of a magpie or the rusty croak of a raven.

At home, the chickadees, both boreal and black-capped, and the woodpeckers were around. The woodpecker has a strange system of flying—a couple of wing-flaps, rest and coast, losing altitude, then flap, flap, up again, coast again, swoop, swoop . . .

The hairy woodpecker was a little out of favor with me today. He had taken up tap-tapping for flies in the gable end of the roof. I flapped and yelled at him but he ignored me, so I tossed an empty peach can up there to get his attention. It worked. He left. But now I suppose the bolder of my acquaintances will ask why I have a peach can on my roof. The more timid will just speculate, which may be worse.

The day ended with a friendly sunset of salmon, gold and mauve.

DECEMBER 2

My friend Lynne and I went to Edmonton last night for a night on the town (pretty wild; we were both tired out and ready to hit the hay by ten-thirty) before my presentation to a library group today. The city is a fine place to visit. I enjoyed shopping in the dressed-for-Christmas malls and I had a good time at the conference, but was I tired as we rolled down the endless miles of Highway 2 toward home!

It had been nice in Edmonton, not much snow and relatively

warm, but as we came south, a huge chinook arch opened its arms in the southwestern sky, a beacon that stayed light and welcoming long after the rest of the world was dark.

I arrived home to four eager "furs" assembled on the porch. We all rushed into the house, had a bite to eat and collapsed into our respective spots, too tired to do another thing.

So endeth my adventure in the fast lane!

DECEMBER 3

Now *this* is my idea of winter! About 50°F and brilliant sunshine. I sat on the boardwalk against the south side of the house for a while, no jacket, soaking up sun, listening to water from the melting snow on the roof run down the drainpipes, and re-reading *Gone with the Wind*. Sometimes I think I should have been born in the Old South—except that women didn't have much fun, spending their lives corsetted to the gills and trying to act helpless and ladylike!

DECEMBER 4

I walked up to the high field through the thick woods today. Game tracks everywhere! So many tracks you'd think it was a cow pasture, but all these tracks belonged to moose, deer and elk. I didn't see any of the track-makers, though I did see two owls swoop silently to deeper cover as I passed.

DECEMBER 5

This morning, as I drove to school in the mild, moist dawn, a coyote flashed across the road ahead of me, a streak of fur with eyes that shone amber in the truck lights. Then he was gone. He looked well-furred and prosperous. I wish him well this winter. Coyotes have a hard life. They seem to be everyone's whipping boy. People blame them just for being coyotes. Surely their behavior is no less honorable than ours would be if we had to scrounge a living on the edge of starvation, hunted for fun and profit. We all do what we have to do to survive.

The weather is wonderful! It has rained for most of the day. Everything smells wet and springy.

December 6

I woke to the radio giving the long-range forecast—less precipitation than usual in December. Prospects poor for a white Christmas. Okay. I can handle that. I stumble out of bed and open the door to let The Prince and Missy in for breakfast—and blink as I look out into thickly falling snow. Odd world we live in.

It's a soft, warm muffling snow. Just above my north corner, in his usual territory, I catch a glimpse of the owl again, silently winging through the snowy forest. He, too, looks soft, warm, muffled. A perfect inhabitant of today's environment.

December 7

Yesterday's snow ended by noon and the afternoon was bright and shiny. But the night was a little colder than we've been having. Today is heavy and sleepy with mostly cloudy skies and a kind of sickly chinook arch in the west.

The birds think that the weather is going to change. The window shelf is alive with chickadees, loudly chickadee-ing as they pick up sunflower seeds. They fly to the lilac bush and, holding the seeds under one foot, pick open the shells, devour the seeds and come rushing back for another load.

On top of the truck cab sits The Prince with his sanctimonious owl expression, watching with great interest as all those lovely "chicken dinners" go flitting by, so near and yet so far!

December 9

A lovely, sleepy Saturday morning. I laze over a cup of coffee, The For-Once-Not-Wicked Prince purring softly in my lap. The only other sounds are the drowsy humming of the furnace and the chickadee-ing of the birds outside the window.

DECEMBER 10

The coldest morning for a long while (0°F) brings out the hungry birds. I sit at the table watching the by-play between the blue jays and the chickadees, competing for sunflower seeds. The blue jays still regard me as the ogre, a veritable fly-in-the-ointment as far as their breakfast goes. It takes several minutes of reconnaissance flights, aborted landings and dithering before one finally lands, scowling fiercely at me, and takes a seed away. The chickadees scatter in the blue jay's path like tiny Cessnas being menaced by a Russian MIG but the scramble is only temporary. The second the jay leaves, little black heads pop out of the bushes and, one after another, the squadron of chickadees comes in for a landing. There are three eating together right now, a miracle of cooperation for these quarrelsome little critters.

As I sit here with birds on my brain, I have a cat at my feet. Timothy is giving my toes one of his regular treatments, rubbing his jowls back and forth over them, hard. Apparently cats have scent glands in their cheeks so I suppose he must be claiming ownership. Listen up, you other cats. The lady's toes belong to *me*. Weird cat!

DECEMBER 11

The Alberta weather has been at it again. Last night the temperature started dropping fast. I scurried around, battening down the igloo: banking the house fires, stoking up the water tank heater and even getting out the extension cord to plug the truck in (just one more of winter's loathsome chores).

By bedtime it was -10°F. I snuggled in with my warm electric blanket over me and The Warm Electric Prince beside me. I expected -20° or worse by morning.

At a quarter-to-six The Prince woke me, announcing that he would go out now. Fool, I thought, glancing at the thermometer. It was 20°, just as I had feared. I looked again. It was *plus* 20°F. A chinook had swept back in overnight. I have only one question. How did The Prince know?

Tonight, as I put the cats out for pre-bed air, it's a beautiful 20°F night with a full moon shining through a gauze curtain of clouds.

DECEMBER 12

Today, as I walked down the road, a great gray owl was perched at the roadside on a delicate treetop that bent with his weight. He watched my approach, his flat-disc face rotating with indecision, his huge, yellow eyes regarding me with his stern-professor look. Then, tucking his heavy-feathered legs beneath him, he rose on silent wings and was gone.

Three beautiful mule deer stood in the middle of the road as I drove out to go to school this morning.

DECEMBER 13

What a weird and wonderful day of weather! The morning was cloudy and just below freezing. Then, in the afternoon, it snowed for two or three hours. Now, in the evening, I sit peacefully by the fire, listening to the soothing sound of water trickling down the drainpipes as the snow on the roof melts again in 33°F temperatures.

A good day for wildlife. A white-tail bounded across the field as I came up with the tractor to feed the cows. Later on, in the softly falling snow, I saw the owl again, perched in the same tree and peering through the snow with his great yellow fog lamps.

DECEMBER 15

I knew that we would pay for rain in December. Today it turned colder and the roads, the yard, the world, turned into a skating rink.

DECEMBER 16

A Christmas card winter day. In the 20s F and starting to snow as evening comes. Marilyn and Ken and their nineteen-year-old daughter, Carolyn, and sixteen-year-old son, Michael, came out. We drove west past the Nitche Valley, almost to the Big Red River, to get a Christmas tree. That was our old riding country when Marilyn and I were kids. It's still beautiful out there, but times have changed, and not necessarily for the better. Now it's easily accessible by truck.

We found two nice trees—tops, actually, so I hope the rest of the tree will continue to grow.

After loading them, we walked another mile or more to the south edge of the still-open Big Red, and stood by the rushing clean green water, speculating on what we would do if we were explorers who had to get across. We decided that we'd have to undress and try to wade it—but we were just as glad not to be faced with that prospect today.

DECEMBER 17

It's snowing, a fine, charmless, businesslike snow, and it's cold (8°F). A plain, nasty winter day. The cows, after several days of contented rustling in the fields, were lined up for welfare first thing this morning.

The cats are three fur circles on the furniture, conserving heat and energy. I've been cold ever since I was out to feed the cows three hours ago so I pace back and forth between the ends of the house, feeding the woodstoves. If that doesn't do the trick, I pause halfway between and turn the furnace thermostat a little higher.

The birds are stocking up against the cold night to come—three chickadees on the window ledge for oatmeal and a downy woodpecker on the sack of fat above.

DECEMBER 20

The weather has been on a downhill slide all week. Tonight it has bottomed out (I hope). It is -30°F. Even the house creaks and groans in protest of this kind of cold. I agree with them. It is *too* cold! Even warm and cosy in the house I am miserable. I worry about the possibility of frozen sewer pipes, tractor breakdowns (the hydraulics move the loader with painful slowness; metal makes brittle sounds). I worry about trucks that might not start, about what will happen if there's a power failure. But most of all, I worry about all the homeless creatures with no warm and safe place to go on a night like this.

My Nordic blood should thrive on cold but somewhere my genes have gone wrong. My soul yearns for the feel of hot sun on my skin.

DECEMBER 21

Officially the first day of winter, and it *is* winter. The temperature slipped still lower overnight. It was sitting at almost -35°F this morning. It was the kind of morning when no sensible animal would crawl out of its den. But of course, people are not sensible animals, so it was business as usual. I drove to town through a frozen world, a world that grew still colder as I came down into the valley of the Big Red. Sundre was a mystery town, afloat in ice fog.

At home, it was a day of feeding, stoking and surviving. Strangely, though, in spite of this intense cold, the creek is flooding. My dad always said that was a sign that a chinook was on its way.

DECEMBER 22

Dad was right about the creek. By noon the temperature was above freezing. A change of more than sixty degrees Fahrenheit in just over twenty-four hours. The air has a whole new, damp spring smell. It "rains" in the woods as snow melts from the tree branches.

With the coming of "spring" I decided to feed the cows in the field again instead of having them hanging around in the woods behind the barn. I also decided that, with easy weather here for a while, the cows had better have a second-class bale of hay. Having made all these momentous decisions, I put a rained-on bale on the loader and headed for the field. The cows followed. I spread the hay for them in the field and set out for home, half a mile away.

As I was closing the Quonset doors after putting the tractor away, I heard a sound. It sounded like a cow. I looked up the trail I had just come down. Indeed, it *was* a cow. It was *all* the cows, marching purposefully, single file, down the trail home, bawling all the way and looking like the offended matrons of the Harper Valley PTA.

If cows could write, I know they'd have been carrying signs that said WE DON'T EAT SECOND-CLASS HAY.

Sorry girls, but, once in a while, you *do*.

I went on about my business. By tomorrow, that hay will be gone.

DECEMBER 23

The first day of Christmas holidays. I celebrate it by having my most excellent sleep of the year. Both The Prince and Morris chose to spend the night outside so I was not awakened by the patter of little feet across my body.

Actually, I awake to the ringing of the phone. I'm in the middle of a fascinating dream about exploring an old log cabin and am amazed that the cabin has a phone—which is ringing.

Nevertheless, I reach full consciousness by the time I reach the phone, and answer as though I've been up for hours. I finally check my watch and find it's just eight-thirty.

DECEMBER 25

A lovely, warm (32°F), peaceful Christmas morning with a windowsill full of chickadees.

Last night I had a houseful of family and friends for a huge ham supper. Then, after everyone was gone, Missy and I walked out to the road and absorbed the beauty and serenity of the silent night.

This afternoon, just at dark, I drove home from feeding my holidaying neighbors' pets. Something was on the road, just beyond my gateway. I drove on up for a closer look. It was a young moose, down on its knees, nosing around in the dirt. As I drove nearer, it finally stood up. It seemed perfectly healthy. I guess it must have been just saying a Christmas prayer—either that or licking up traces of salt the road-sanding crew left behind!

DECEMBER 26

After all the Christmas rush it's wonderful to have a nothing-in-particular day. I promise myself that I will write. Then I kill a lot of time doing every other thing I can think of.

The cats play a joyful game with the discarded edge of my computer paper while their Christmas present (a $4.99 plush mouse with a bell on its tail and with "cat-attracting scent") lies totally ignored in the middle of the floor.

DECEMBER 27

A mild gray day. Calgary was the warmest spot in Canada today. I brought in some wood since it was supposed to snow. It rained instead. Crazy country.

DECEMBER 28

It did get around to a little snow overnight—maybe half an inch of gentle wet white stuff that clings to everything it touches. Each poplar tree wears a wide white stripe down its west side where the snow came in on the west wind.

One of my favorite citizens of the woods, the downy woodpecker, was back at the feeder today after a few days' absence. Well-groomed, polite and serene, minding his own business and keeping his beak out of everyone else's business, he is the ideal guest.

Though it's cloudy now, there was bright sun this morning. One gift of these short days is the low sun in the south, pouring through the big front window and drenching the couch in its warmth. None of "us cats" can resist it. The Prince and I curled up together there for a while and cuddled and purred. Back-lighted by the sun, he is magnificent with each whisker and hair turned into a miniature, glowing light-saber.

I reach out and scratch his furry jowls, admiring as always the wonderful, delicate bone structure of a cat's face. (Having approximately the same facial bone structure as a rice pudding myself, I am fascinated by great cheekbones on *anybody*.)

DECEMBER 30

Another company day. These holidays are endangering my antisocial personality!

Just before sundown, everyone has gone and Missy and I get time for a small woodcutting expedition.

Loaded up—that includes Missy, standing proudly in the back of the battered, twelve-year-old farm truck—I drive out of the woods and stop to open the barnyard gate. As I get out of the truck, I glimpse a perfect portrait: Missy, against the sunset sky, her head up, eyes aglow with the excitement of the ride, her eager breathing puffing little clouds of steam into the cool evening air.

There is something so essentially "dog" about the way she looks just now, so happy over nothing, asking only to come with me, to be my dog and to help with whatever I am doing.

It's no secret that cats are my first love. The aristocrats of creation, so proud, elegant, calm and in charge, favoring us with their affection through a sense of noblesse oblige, perhaps.

But, no society can function with aristocrats alone. It needs its loyal, steady and unquestioning peasants. Those are the dogs, standing ever nearby, waiting to serve.

Speaking of being nearby, as another demonstration of her total affection, I presume, Missy has taken to following so closely behind me on the narrow trails through the snow that, with every step, her hard rubber nose jabs me in the calf. Some may call this devotion. I call it bruising.

DECEMBER 31

The last day of the year—and of a decade. There is something sad about endings. A sense of loss. A feeling that no matter how you used the time, it wasn't good enough. You should have lived more, felt more, given more, taken more. It's a feeling that grows as the years pile up and becomes particularly insistent when you realize, as I do at the end of this decade, that the first half of your life, the golden, careless years of youth, is gone. Despite the rewards of maturity, the slope must now be downward.

But maybe that's wrong. Maybe life isn't a mountain with a long climb to a narrow peak and then a steep descent into the valley of age. Maybe, instead, the climb brings us to a wide plateau, comfortable with achievement and high enough to view the world in its true perspective. A place from which to analyze our priorities in time to spend the second half of our lives on the things that really matter to us.

My father was the age I am now when I was born, but it never once seemed to me that he was over the hill, the best part of his life already lived by the time I knew him. He lived twenty-nine more years and, in that time, put so much good into my life.

I bring myself out of my reverie and look forward, seeing all the little signs and portents of the day.

On an afternoon walk through the snowy woods I spot a black dot moving purposefully across the snow. A tiny spider. Shouldn't he be either dead or deep in some cosy cranny at this time of year? Apparently not. Circumstances did not rule his life. *He* was in charge. Not a bad thought for the new year.

Tonight, as I drove home from a New Year's Eve visit, a sudden flash of white skittered across the road in front of me. I glanced into the ditch, expecting to see a white cat on his nocturnal prowl. But, no. It's a rabbit! A white rabbit! (I'm beginning to sound like Alice in Wonderland.) I was amazed. Rabbits have been scarce in this country lately. I haven't seen one for years. I miss them. They are an important link in the food chain but they also should be here just because they *are* rabbits and we ought to have some!

So, at the dawn of a decade, a white rabbit. What does it mean? Are white rabbits the opposite of black cats, and therefore good luck? (Actually, all cats are good luck to me.) Is this the beginning of a resurgence of rabbits? Or perhaps the year of the rabbit? Who knows. I drove the rest of the way home under a starry sky, the big dipper right there where I watched it in my childhood. The universe is no doubt unfolding as it should.

Last year on New Year's Eve, I stayed home and, tired, went to bed at eleven. Fifteen minutes later, as I lay reading, the doorbell rang. What now? Someone had been celebrating too well and gone off the road? I threw on my housecoat and went warily to the door. Not a soul in sight. Except for Missy. Spotting me, she stood upright, feet against the door jamb, wanting to come in for the night. This time her paw just barely missed connecting with the doorbell button!

JANUARY 1

Startling news! 1990 doesn't feel any different than 1989.

JANUARY 2

I wanted to sit and read undisturbed for five minutes this morning. Timothy wanted attention. I trekked through the house to find a peaceful spot. Valiantly, Timothy stumped along behind, trailing me from room to room. I took refuge in my bedroom, flopping down on my stomach on the bed to read the newspaper.

There is a sudden commotion. Scrambling wildly, Timothy launches himself onto the bed, no small feat for an elderly, overweight, three-legged gentleman. (Tim has been a "triped" for more than ten years now. He crawled home from a spring night's hunting with a hind leg crippled. Although the only visible damage was a small puncture wound in his "elbow" joint, the vet said his ligaments were ruined and the leg would have to be amputated. I never did find out what caused the injury, but suspected an owl had tried to pick him up, found him too heavy and dropped him. The owl probably got a hernia for his punishment.) Callously, I ignore him and go on reading. Desperately wanting to be held, he studies the situation and finally solves the problem by climbing on top of me and lying comfortably sprawled across my back.

I continue reading with determination. There is another thud on the bed. The Prince has arrived. He snuggles down at my side, happily kneading my armpit with his sharp claws.

Enough, boys, I surrender! I turn over and cuddle Timothy on my lap while keeping one arm around The Prince. Both cats purr loudly, out of rhythm with each other. We (well, at least two of us) have found perfect bliss.

JANUARY 3

I have never envied people their small children. My "fur family" is usually so much easier on the nerves than screaming babies and terrible two-year-olds.

I said "usually." Today was an exception. As I sat by the fire trying to write a letter, in swaggered The Prince, tail at attention, in search of trouble. He found it. A big clumsy fly had awakened and was buzzing on the window. This required immediate action. The Prince launched himself onto the table and, in pursuit of the fly, engaged the open-weave curtains in mortal combat. Just as he was considering a trip *up* the curtains, he stepped on a plastic bag that was lying on the edge of the table, slipped and fell on the floor. It was wonderful! Prince, the consummate, cocksure athlete, landing on his derriere just like any of us other mortals might. At the risk of grave feline censure—a laughed-at cat can pout at considerable length—I laughed uproariously. But not for long. It's hard to laugh when an overweight cat is making an earnest attempt to climb your leg. Timothy had arrived and, finding the angle impossible for a jump into my lap, was traversing my calf with more energy than finesse.

While disengaging my flesh from his claws, I glanced out the window—just in time to see Missy execute a splendid broken-field run across the yard and make a touchdown, carrying the green blanket she had just stolen from the bench on the deck.

I sighed. Today, it was worse than having kids. And to think, they'll never grow up and send flowers on Mother's Day!

Missy sleeps just as hard at night as she plays during the day. Sacked out flat on her side she lies in deep sleep. Her eyes, not quite tight shut, flip rapidly back and forth. This must be the stuff dreams are made of, the famous REM sleep.

She looks almost comatose, her mouth slightly agape, long, pink tongue tucked neatly between her fangs. She snores. Her feet jerk spasmodically. Her nose twitches . . .

And visions of Porterhouse dance through her head.

JANUARY 4

A heavy, heavy gray day. About 20°F with a chinook struggling unsuccessfully to be born.

I cut and hauled a few days' supply of wood. Then, just at dusk, I took a short walk south of the yard to see if anything interesting was to be found on such a dull day. The chickadees were. The treetops were alive with them as they foraged for supper. As I turned toward home, I caught a glimpse of something else: two plump grouse, each perched in the highest branches of a poplar tree. What a contrast to the quick, acrobatic chickadees! The grouse looked so staid and matronly that I could hardly believe they'd actually flown up there. I kept worrying that they might fall and hurt themselves.

JANUARY 5

The chinook finally broke through. It's warm outside but I almost froze to death in the house this morning. Strange how it often seems cold inside when it's warming up outside.

I cleaned out my old emergency supply of square bales that I keep on hand in case of a tractor breakdown. Big round bales weigh about a thousand pounds. Obviously, they can't be handled without machinery. Square bales weight just forty or fifty pounds so I keep a few on hand. This bunch had been in the Quonset for several years and were looking the worse for wear, so I fed them to the cows and made room for a fresh supply.

For the first couple of years after Dad died and I took over running the place, I fed just square bales, at least fifteen every day, heaved onto the back of the truck and thrown out to the cows each afternoon, after a full day of teaching.

Now, I was amazed at how much work it was to haul out these few bales. I felt quite sorry for myself as I wrestled with the awkward, prickly brutes! Could I go back to doing this every day? It would seem a lot harder now (surely being ten years older doesn't have anything to do with it!). But then, everything seems hard as soon as you've tried doing it the easy way.

I can remember (barely) the days when there was no electricity in this part of the country. (No, I'm not *that* old, but in the fifties this was real back country.) I can clearly remember getting indoor plumbing a few years after the power. Our first telephone came in about 1964.

And yet, in the years before we had any of those things, we never felt underprivileged. UNICEF never mounted campaigns to help us poor little waifs heading for outdoor biffys when it was -40°F!

We survived. We thrived.

What will the kids of the nineties remember? Being the last family on the block to get a CD player? Everything is relative, I guess.

JANUARY 7

A rip-roaring chinook blew for most of the day. Usually I don't mind a little wind—probably because in this notch in the trees I hardly ever feel it—but today as I took the cows' bale across the field I felt like I'd blow away, tractor and all. The wind blew my hair into my eyes and scrambled my brains.

Later, Marilyn and Ken and I went for a walk to enjoy the sunshine and check on the Scruffy bull who looks a little moth-eaten and might need some louse treatment. We went on to check the spring where the cows have been drinking. It was fine, lots of water.

Then, of course, I had to explore. There was another little frozen-over pothole in the below-the-spring swamp that I just *had* to stomp on and break open so the cows would have another drinking place. I tromped on the little circle of ice with all my weight (a force to be reckoned with!). My foot went through the ice and just kept on going right through the ooze underneath, over my boot-top, past my knee, all the way up my thigh! I guess I'd still be going straight for China but my other foot was still on dry land and I finally high-centered on a hummock. There I sat, laughing hysterically, one leg on dry land and the other one drowned in the swamp.

Under the circumstances, it seemed best to declare the day's explorations complete. I reefed my bedraggled leg back to join the remainder of my body and squelched off for home.

When I let the animals out this evening I stepped out into a mild moonlit night with a skyful of stars shining through wisps of clouds that hurried eastward on the wings of the wind.

JANUARY 9

I was about an hour later than usual getting out with feed today. Apron was not in the least inconvenienced by this. I found her in the bale yard helping herself to the smorgasbord. Scruffy had pushed his head and shoulders through the fence and was also dining off a convenient bale.

JANUARY 10

The chinook is hanging on. We haven't had below-zero weather since December 21.

This morning I awoke to a star-studded sky and a half inch of fresh snow that had come in on the west wind last night. The wind was still sighing in the woods this morning and it stayed at work all day. By midafternoon the snow was sculpted and polished till it shone like fresh-starched and pressed laundry. A clean, crisp world.

The grouse was foraging on the hillside above the creek today.

JANUARY 11

A slightly colder day but bright and sunny and still comfortably above zero and bright and sunny.

Driving to school today, I could see day coming to the sky. In the gray-blue western sky, the moon, full and perfect—so clear I could see its mountain ranges—still reigned. To the east, the sky gradually lighted and brightened, the eastern horizon turning a soft orange-beige with the light of the almost-risen sun.

I noticed an extra few minutes of daylight today. Another month and the days will race, out of control, toward the equinox and on to the longest day.

JANUARY 12

Friday, at last! And that's what's wrong with working—I mean working in the formal five-days-a-week sense. We wish our lives away and pass over hundreds of wonderful days, just trying to get through them, to last until another weekend. No wonder Thoreau said that most people live lives of quiet desperation.

This first week back at work after Christmas holidays I've done quite well about getting up early so I'll have plenty of time to get ready to go, but today I don't want to hurry. It's a mild morning, just below freezing, with the chinook re-exerting control. As I stepped out on the porch to let the dog in I felt the touch of the gentle wind, heard the hum of a vehicle on the main road, distance-softened to a friendly sound, and saw the dawn subtly graying the dark eastern sky. It was a peaceful moment, one I didn't want to interrupt to go and try to do *something* with my hair.

Who was it that said, "What is this life so full of care we have no time to stand and stare?"

It was a day of skies. Beginning with a sunrise that glowed like molten metal and by noon turned part brilliant blue and part chinook cloud of a dozen colors—dark, dark gray-blue, sun-touched pearl gray, pale pink and everything in between.

It was also a day of birds. Chickadees everywhere, flitting around the feeders like piranhas in a feeding frenzy. So many and so frenetic that just watching them was tiring. Chickadees are really the most aggressive birds. They can hardly take time to eat, they're so busy chasing each other away from the feed. They remind me of some small, sweet-faced kids I've taught. They look so young and innocent that they get away with murder. Likewise the chickadees. If they were the size of crows and behaved like chickadees, shotguns would come out all over the world!

The downy woodpecker paid a visit to the bag of fat, his serenity a welcome contrast to the belligerence of the chickadees.

The flock of Hungarian partridges were in their usual territory along the north road. Coming home from Sundre in the late afternoon, I was rewarded by the sight of two different owls. One, a small gray type I couldn't identify, was perched on a neighbor's TV antenna. Half a mile farther on, in his usual territory, the great gray sat on a fencepost, his head swivelling as he checked out mousing prospects.

A space in today's hall of fame—no, make that shame—must be saved for the cows. Back in the bales again! Twenty or more of them in there this time, making a real mess. They came in from a new side today (this makes three out of four sides of the fence they've attacked). Why, I don't know. They're not hungry. They had a perfectly good feed yesterday, and I wasn't late today. I think they're doing it out of sheer devilment. Looks like I'll have to get some help and do some major fence-reinforcing tomorrow. But, cows, listen carefully. If you don't like the rules around here, I'll find you someplace else to go. Have you heard of a place called McDonald's? I understand they need a lot of cows in their business . . .

JANUARY 13

The blue jays are back. Four of them sweeping down to see what they can pillage. Ha! Ha! The dog's dish is empty. But they have a shot at the cracked corn (I think) on the window ledge, diving in for quick forays and taking off when they see my dreaded face. Hey, guys, relax. I don't care if you have it. I don't think the chickadees will eat it anyway. I might as well have skipped the wild bird seed mix and stuck to rolled oats, which the chickadees love.

Anyway, the jays manage to get away with a few morsels. Beautiful as they are, they have a poor profile. They look like men with long, sharp noses, low foreheads, greased-down hair and weak chins. Combine this with their shifty-eyed, furtive look when they think they're stealing something, and it's like having a window ledge full of Mafia hit-men!

Their convention doesn't last long. They see that I'm here to stay and suddenly, en masse, they take off, flinging crude remarks at me over their shoulders.

A busy "cowboy" afternoon. The Walkers, my usual crew, came to help and we branded and deloused Scruffy and branded the five replacement heifers and a little "deep freeze" steer. I'd been keeping the calves in the bull corral since weaning in October and now it was time to let them out and lock the bulls up until breeding season in May. I also put the Apron cow into the slammer. She's the ringleader in all this breaking and entering the cows have been into lately.

After we finished with the cattle we fed the herd behind the barn and then we all trekked up to the field to repair the bale corral *again*. This time we did it up in style, all the wires retightened and a row of *boards* all the way around.

Instead of staying back to eat their hay, the whole herd trailed up to the field behind us and took up a position a hundred yards away to watch the whole repair process. As they stood all bunched up and staring balefully (believe it or not, that pun is accidental), I could almost hear the vibes . . .

"Watch carefully now, girls, if we see how they put it together, we'll know how to take it apart . . ."

JANUARY 14

A soft gray morning with an occasional white feather floating from the sky. The woods were deep with peace. Nothing stirred, but the patterns of tracks showed that I was not alone out there.

The cows did *not* get in the hay. But now there's a new development. Four of the five calves branded and let out yesterday have gone into hiding somewhere. Only one was with the rest of the cattle at feeding time. Oh well, I guess they'll come out when they get hungry.

Just before dusk there is a commotion in the sky, just at treetop level. Woodpeckers, from two different directions, laughing excitedly to each other. Suddenly, from the west comes a loud RAT-A-TAT. One of the birds has landed and is sending out drum signals.

What is the meaning of all this communication? It's too early for mating, isn't it? Maybe spring is closer than we think.

The Prince has a built-in radar. He can tell instantly when I'm busy. If I sit down intending to write I can expect him to land in my lap within seconds. And, of course, when I don't have time for him he's at his most charming, lying in a downy-soft semicircle, front paws on my arm, and looking up at me with those luminous green eyes. How can you possibly resist me, ask those eyes.

I can't.

JANUARY 15

Still mild but cloudy by midafternoon. Coyotes were howling to each other from two directions in broad daylight. That doesn't happen very often. Does it mean a change in the weather, or just that they felt like howling? The forecast promises the possibility of a little snow.

While splitting wood I found two specimens of "many-legged black wood bugitula" hibernating under the bark. I felt a little badly, dislodging them from their cosy home, so I was careful not to squash them but pushed them gently into a sheltered cranny. I doubt that they'll survive but all may not be lost. Some enterprising bird may find a surprise supper waiting for his probing beak. These wood-dwelling bugs are no doubt one motivation for the woodpeckers' busy hammering.

The middle of January and not quite dark at five-thirty. We're edging out of the darkness.

January 16

Snow flurries and a bit colder. The calves came home! As I walked through the barnyard to get the tractor, I saw the four of them galloping, tails up, from the southwest to join the assembled herd. The youngsters must have just holed up and pouted in the woods for a couple of days. They're perfectly happy, and hungry, now!

January 17

The thermometer edged down last night and I was afraid it might hit 0°F, spoiling the run of above-zero days (now twenty-six). But it didn't. It was 10°F when I got up.

It turned into a beautiful blue and crystal winter day, every twig a filigree of frost standing out against an azure sky.

January 18

I saw the smaller owl again, the one who was on the neighbor's TV antenna a few days ago. He was still in the same area so he must be a resident.

January 19

At seven in the morning the quarter moon is still in a black sky outside the kitchen window. Pure, cold and seemingly unattainable, she is always serene, unmoved by the frantic race below her.

Back on earth, things were a little tense for a while as the water from the old flowing well down at the barnyard had stopped running into the stock-watering tank. This water, moving only by its own artesian pressure, is piped a hundred feet underground from well to tank. There's no way to pump it from its source, no way to get at its source, other than by heavy-duty digging. If something major went wrong now with the creek still frozen solid for another three months . . .

Ken came and diagnosed the problem. The tank, heaving with the frost, had shifted position, pinching the plastic intake hose enough to almost stop the flow. The slowdown was enough to cause a few inches of the pipe to freeze solid. A kettlefull of hot water thawed it out and minor adjustments took the kink out of the pipe.

I breathe a sigh of relief—and a prayer of gratitude that the solution was so simple, that the problem didn't hit on some -40°F day and for friends who are always there to lend a hand.

I'm tired tonight, partly from running around helping with the tank-thawing, partly from being able to relax now that the problem is solved and partly just because it's been a "heavy" day. The chinook is still around but it seems to have trapped some cooler air in an inversion. Smoke, trying to rise from smouldering brush piles, travels more horizontally than vertically. My wood fire has sulked along unproductively all day.

Even the animals are tired. They collapsed in four fur circles before supper and for hours breathing was exercise enough for them.

JANUARY 20

A mild, gray day with temperatures at about the melting point.

I spend an hour or two getting some wood out of the bush. At first it seems so quiet and deserted out there but the forest people are around. As I drive down the narrow trail the great gray owl swoops out of nowhere on his silent wings and disappears into nowhere again, seeking solitude. If I could speak owl I would apologize for my intrusion.

Later, as I load my wood, I am joined by a cheerful pair of whisky jacks foraging among the branches above me. Nearby a happy squirrel sits chittering on a branch, teasing Missy.

Missy is having a wonderful time. While I saw wood she disappears somewhere. Ten minutes later she comes walloping back through the woods, tongue hanging out, a big grin on her face. She rushes up to me, eyes aglow, and proceeds to tell me about all the wonderful things she's seen. A minute later, she's gone again.

Animals could teach us a valuable lesson about being happy. As long as she gets something to eat and has her person around, Missy's whole life is a joyous adventure.

The Prince, too, is a master at the art of entertainment. His games can be quite complex, requiring a plan.

Today, as I came up from the barnyard, he was sitting on a fence post just below the bridge. I stopped and offered him a ride home on my shoulder. He was noncommittal in his answer so I set him on my shoulder, walked a couple of steps and then stopped. He stepped back onto the fence, thus declining the ride. It wasn't part of his plan.

Missy and I went on across the bridge and started up the hill. All of a sudden, a furry bullet shot past my feet: The Prince, tail stiff as a rudder, rocketing up the hill past us. Of course, just as The Prince had planned, Missy immediately gave chase, narrowing the gap excitingly until, just in the nick of time, the cat leapt into the rafters of the small abandoned greenhouse at the edge of the lawn. There he sat, fluffed up like a porcupine, laughing down at the dog and intensely pleased with the scenario he had just invented, directed, starred in—and even done his own stunts in!

JANUARY 21

A beautiful sunny Sunday with snow melting gently off the roof. A walk in the woods found three friendly whisky jacks who asked if I hadn't brought along a bite to eat, one loudly squawking blue jay and three recently excavated squirrel larders. One diggings had at least nine little mine shafts and all were surrounded by huge piles of debris left behind when the squirrels ate the seeds from the spruce cones and discarded the hulls.

Who says animals and humans are different? We all leave a trail of garbage behind us, but at least the squirrels' garbage is biodegradable.

JANUARY 22

A mild, melting day. When I fed the cows a coyote was in the field with them, the cattle and the much-maligned predator peacefully coexisting a hundred yards apart.

I cut wood for an hour this afternoon with treetops full of spring-singing chickadees above me.

JANUARY 23

A steady, gentle snowfall started just before daylight. It lasted for an hour or two, then changed to sunshine by noon, followed by more clouds. A little of everything. But no cold! We've made it through a month of deepest winter without the temperature going below 0°F.

JANUARY 25

What are the mysterious silent conversations that pass between animals? This morning The Wicked Prince came in, had a snack and then walked over to where Timothy was lying and commenced to wash Tim's head as gently and assiduously as a conscientious valet. Tim smiled and accepted this service for several minutes till, all of a sudden, ears went flat, paws came up and love turned to war. Why? You'll have to ask the cats.

JANUARY 26

Saw two coyotes hunting in the field today. Missy went racing off to investigate, but when I whistled she called off the encounter quite willingly. Even she probably senses that two against one is bad politics.

JANUARY 27

A colder (15°F) somber, gray morning. Still, the advance of daylight makes itself felt. Even on this sunless morning the lights can go out by nine.

Everything is very quiet. Only peaceful Saturday-morning sounds. The furnace hums reassuringly, the clock ticks, Missy, sound asleep on her rug—except for head and front paws on the good carpet—sighs with content occasionally. Outside, a few notes of chickadee song. A blue jay and a whisky jack, cousins, make a foray to check for worthy snacks. Fooled you, guys. The dog's dish is *in*.

I come into the porch with an armful of wood and a gust of warm air from the woodstove rushes to meet me. Simultaneously, the smell of simmering stew floats out from the kitchen. For a second, I am immersed in a wave of total contentment. It makes me think how much happiness the human animal misses by insisting on complexity in life. Why shouldn't warmth and the promise of a good meal on a cold winter day be reason enough to enjoy just being alive? We would truly realize the value of these simple things only if we lost them.

By noon the sky had cleared and a rip-snorting gale came up. It was a good thing I was the only traffic as I hauled a bale across the field because my mane blew across my eyes so that I could barely see where I was going.

Two fruitless but funny chases took place today. A big fly wakened in the sunshine and began to bumble back and forth across the inside of the window, much to the delight of a chickadee who began to hop wildly back and forth on the windowsill outside, in hot pursuit. Poor bird. I'm sure he blamed his bifocals for his inability to lay his beak on that obviously reachable, but totally untouchable, fly.

Later, as Missy and I walked across the barnyard in the racing wind, a piece of tarpaper tore loose from the old house that is being torn down and went skittering across the snow, just at ground level. Instantly, Missy took up the chase, only to stop and stare, disappointed, at the lifeless thing that came to rest on the snow. I'm sure she thought she was after one of those pesky ravens again.

The day turned a little sad in midafternoon. Marilyn and I walked up to the south quarter to check on the horses who are rustling on the hayfields for the winter. Angel, Flame, Copper and Rainy were all fat—too fat for this time of year. But our first look at Red was a shock. Since I'd last seen her close up, a month ago, she'd become terribly thin, in such poor shape that there was no way she would last out the winter.

In a way, it was no surprise. She was past thirty. Two falls ago I had thought she was looking kind of rough so I got her in with the intention of having her put down. But, she talked me out of it. She looked at me with eyes that still burned with the fire of living and I knew positively then that she didn't want to die—not yet. I turned her out with the others and she perked up and had been fine ever since. Until now.

Again it was time to call on Jim Haug, my closest neighbor and good friend to come with a rifle. He doesn't kill because he enjoys killing. Far from it. He is a truly gentle man who loves and respects all creatures great and small. He told me once how he no longer kills coyotes because of the dying look the last one he shot gave him many years ago. The thought of killing another leaves him haunted by that look of accusation. Jim kills for mercy or necessity, and when he kills, he kills well.

Red died instantly from a bullet in her head, still crunching a final mouthful of oats. I watched her go down. It seemed the least I could do. It was as good a way to die as a horse—or a human—could ask for. In some ways we are kinder to horses than people. If she had been human we would have put her in a hospital bed, attached her to machines and dragged her death out miserably. As it was, she died proud.

My regrets about Red are contradictory. I probably waited too long. I shouldn't have let her get so thin. And yet, I know she hadn't given up. Even skin and bones she was still bright-eyed and wary. Faithful to the role she played all her life, she refused to be caught. When she saw the halter she cantered off, fighting for her freedom. She still didn't want to die. And maybe she would have hung on a few more weeks. I could have brought her in, kept her in the barn and fed her specially. And she would have hated it. She wanted to be free. Now she is.

JANUARY 29

It had to happen. The weather finally went bad on us. It started last night with a little snow and an icy wind and by morning it was below zero. So ends a month and five days of above-zero weather.

Today was bright and shiny, the sun doing its best against the biting east wind, but tonight is going to be cold one. I spent the afternoon feeding, bedding, stoking the water tank heater and bringing stacks of wood into the house. Tonight, as always in very cold weather, I'm restless, uneasy. At least the cows aren't due to start calving for another two weeks.

I heard the owl hooting in the north woods just before dark. I could imagine him sitting on a high branch in the deep, dim forest, his feathers fluffed against the cold, his legs cosy in their feathery pajamas. I hope all creatures find a sheltered den this unforgiving night.

JANUARY 30

A truly nasty day. Cloudy with an icy wind. Spitting a fine snow off and on all day. -20°F at four P.M. The Hungarian partridges were along the north road when I came home at noon, fluffed up to twice their usual size.

JANUARY 31

Sunshine but not much rise in temperature all day and a vicious southeast wind. In the few minutes I was on the tractor hauling two bales out to the cows behind the barn, my face was so cold it felt like it might shatter and fall off in little pieces. I spent an hour reading the newspaper under my electric blanket when I got in.

But, earlier, as I walked across the big corral toward the house, I noticed a bunch of cattle marching purposefully toward the creek. I wonder . . .

Delaying my indoor thaw, I hurried over to investigate. Yes! The creek is flooding. And the weather forecast is for warming by Friday.

FEBRUARY 1

Warming up to -10°F. Everything is relative. Last week, that would have been "pretty darn cold." Now, it's quite bearable, especially as I watch the sun setting in a half-formed chinook arch tonight.

I'm tired this evening, looking forward to the time for sleep. I think it's tiredness brought on by the release from the tension of life in the deep cold.

The Prince's reaction is just the opposite. At four A.M. (or some equally uncivilized hour—my eyes were only half open when I checked the clock) he's up and scratching the chair to be let out for the first time in nearly a week. (He *has* been going out quite regularly but this is the first time it's been *his* idea.)

As I stagger back to bed I check the thermometer. Still -10. But by eight o'clock it's 10 above. The Prince comes back in to play wildly for a few minutes with—get this—his $4.99 plush mouse with a bell on its tail and cat-attracting scent!

Not a bird in sight as I eat breakfast. After four days of frantic activity, stuffing their furnaces against the cold, they, too, must be tired and enjoying a sleep-in in their cosy hollow trees.

FEBRUARY 2

I was going to feed the cows in the field but the cows wouldn't follow me. When I got there I found out the reason. Up there, the chinook was blowing gale-force, whipping the latest snow into a stinging blizzard. The cows knew best. I fed them in the woods.

A coyote shot across the road in front of me this afternoon, looking sleek and well-fed. There must be a good mouse-supply this winter.

FEBRUARY 3

A beautiful chinooky, sunny Saturday. At one o'clock it's 45°F on the shady side of the house. The world is lazy and peaceful today with all the animals gratefully accepting the gift of warmth. I take advantage of the day to cut a little wood to have on hand for winter's next siege.

One piece of bad news. My neighbor Jim tells me that the great gray owl who lived at the north corner is dead. Jim saw ravens congregating and went to find out why. The owl was lying dead under a power pole. Probably the victim of a collision with the power line, I would guess.

Why do we have to lose the rare and beautiful things? I'd rather have sacrificed a raven. But, nobody appointed me the judge of life and death, and I'm just as glad they didn't.

As happens once in a while, I have acquired a house-mouse. With only *three* cats in the house, I suppose it's to be expected! But as if it isn't bad enough that the cats don't catch him, to add insult to injury, he *lives* on Cat Chow! Occasionally I have to remove a cache of it from a rarely used sewing machine drawer. So far no luck with trapping him.

It could be worse. I just read in *Time* magazine about a rat who made a nest in the innards of a $107,000 computer in Washington, D.C., filling it with banana peels, corn cobs and a Hostess Twinkie. The computer was a total loss. Stay in the sewing machine drawer please, mouse!

FEBRUARY 4

One of those days to make you believe that clouds really do have a silver lining. The day began gray and damp with a skiff of snow already fallen. Outside was uninviting and it felt chilly in the house. Then, all of a sudden, as I fed the cows at about ten o'clock, the sun broke through into an ever-widening chinook arch. An alchemist had turned the day from lead to gold.

I sit at the table now, with the sunshine streaming through my big, streaky south windows. Chickadees come and go, looking long and sleek, their feathers smooth in the warm air. During the cold days they looked like feather-covered balls.

This afternoon Marilyn and I went cross-country skiing at the Bearberry Nordic Center about twenty-five miles from here. I had never skied on a more perfect day. Warm sun in a brilliant blue sky, contrasting with scurrying clouds in every shade of white and gray, the hills an oil painting in shades of blue, deep gray, and white. We

skied about five miles over competition-class trails through foothills and forest.

FEBRUARY 5

A purple, mauve and pink sunrise, spread around 360 degrees of sky. By noon the chinook was blowing another gale. I drove home down the north road behind an uncovered truckload of grain, which was blowing away in a golden blizzard. I felt a moment's sympathy for the farmer's misfortune but then another thought crossed my mind. What a lucky windfall (pun intended this time) for the struggling little band of Hungarian partridges trying to make a living along this windswept road!

Nature never lets anything go to waste. Although her methods aren't always pretty, she is the ultimate recycler. The ravens ate the owl. From the chorus of howls in the south quarter last week, I'm sure a whole convention of coyotes celebrated the inheritance of a horse carcass in the depths of winter. And why shouldn't they celebrate? The horse is beyond suffering. It is only right that her remains return to the great cycle of nature. Her death is the gift of life for those who feed on her. When the coyotes die their bodies will someday become soil where rich grass will grow to feed a new generation of horses.

FEBRUARY 9

It's been a busy week, spent organizing courses for a new semester, working on a novel and getting together a presentation for a teachers' convention in Red Deer.

Today, it was up at the crack of dawn—actually, dawn hadn't even considered cracking yet—and on the road to Red Deer by seven. It was a good day, meeting interesting people and being treated with more respect than I deserved, but by the time I was finished at two o'clock, I was ready to go home.

Like a homing pigeon too long from her coop, and spurred by

visions of my own cosy den in the woods, I urged my poor gutless truck to its best efforts.

Home sweet home, where nobody asks me hard questions and where being able to use a can opener makes me a genius in the eyes of my furry roommates.

A lazy rest of the day, spent doing just the basic chores and regularly sneaking back for another chapter of the Wilbur Smith novel I'm reading.

Daylight lasts long enough to go out after supper now. At six o'clock, though the sun was long set, there was light enough for a walk down the lane with Missy. The sky was fading to gray, a coyote howled in the west and the first star shone in the eastern sky.

FEBRUARY 10

It turned out to be quite a day, full of jobs I had planned to do—and events I hadn't planned on. I brought in two small loads of wood from the pasture—a new cold spell is predicted. Then, since according to the chart the first calf *could* come tomorrow, I decided I'd better put the cows in the big corral. I lured them in with a bale of hay, except for a little group of hard-core independents who preferred not to be lured. They had to be left with the gate open and the feed inside while they made up their minds over the course of the afternoon.

Then, through a variety of circumstances, I found myself with five people (three different sets) for coffee. That was fine. I was glad to see all of them but I did wish that I'd have taken time to straighten out at least the top layer of clutter in the house before taking on the outside jobs!

Somewhere in the middle of all this I did find enough time to save a life—maybe. A brown (boreal) chickadee had a collision with a window. Fortunately all the cats were in the house when I looked out to find Missy peering interestedly into the small space between her house and the big house. Sure enough, the fallen flier was lying there in a crumpled heap. At first I thought he was dead. But, no, his sides were heaving with his fast breathing. Carefully I scooped him up and held him lightly in one hand. His beak was wide open as he gasped for breath and his eyes blinked rapidly. I held him for a few minutes, studying his color. He was three shades of brown, plus gray and charcoal, with just a hint of dingy white under his chin. I ruffled his feathers gently and began to understand how such a tiny package of life can survive at -40°F. He was more feathers than bird. Layer after layer of downy softness, lying so lightly that every bit of body warmth is trapped in the insulating spaces. I never did find my way through the feathers to actually see his skin.

Gradually, his breathing began to slow and he moved a little. I set him on top of the doghouse roof. He skidded a little as his claws were still clenched into tiny black fists, but he gave his wings an experimental twitch, then a flap, and suddenly he took off. He landed among his relatives in the lilac bush, apparently none the worse for wear, but with quite a bedtime story to tell the hollow-tree gang tonight.

FEBRUARY 11

The chickadees are at work outside the window this mild gray morning. They are collecting some kind of tidbits from the seed mixture on the window ledge and carrying them to a lilac branch where they work them over thoroughly with beak and claw.

As I drove to church at ten-forty-five I noticed that the sky had turned dark gray in the west. When I came out of church at twelve-thirty it was sprinkling rain. When I got home ten minutes later it was *really* raining. An hour later it was spitting snow and by mid-afternoon a blizzard was howling through the yard.

I spent a couple of hours battening down the plantation against a stormy night, feeding, stoking, bedding—and hoping no cow would even consider calving tonight.

FEBRUARY 12

The weather is bottoming out again. It will probably hit -20°F tonight, which is *too* cold at calving time.

Around eleven this evening I trek down to the barnyard to stoke the water tank heater and look at the cows. All of them promise they will not have babies tonight. I compliment them on their good sense.

I hate going out late at night like this, putting on all those clothes when I should be crawling into my warm bed. But once out, it's not so bad. Under a half moon and a lot of stars the snow's crunch is high-pitched with cold and an occasional crack sounds from the woods as frost settles deeper into the trees. A few cows munch desultorily on the last of their hay while most are settled cosily into their straw bed, chewing their cuds. We'll survive the night.

FEBRUARY 13

A day that began and ended with a cold trek to check the cows and stoke the tank heater. This morning—pale daylight by seven-fifteen—I walked into a cold dawn. In the east, a frigid pale peach sunrise faded into the west where the moon still rode high in a gray-blue sky.

As I turned out of the lane on my way to school, two deer crossed the road ahead of me and sailed over the fence into the quarter across the road.

The day turned bright and sunny, enough to warm the house without the furnace running for three or four hours, but the outside temperature never even reached 0°F.

The cows are obediently keeping their calves tucked in where it's warm. I stuck one of the more likely-looking heifers in the barn. I don't think she's quite ready, but in this weather it never hurts to be extra cautious.

Right after supper I dived into a hot bath and enjoyed a read and soak. The Prince decided that this was one of those times to regard me in the tub as the eighth wonder of the world. He does this occasionally—comes pussyfooting into the bathroom to stand with his front paws on the edge of the tub, solemnly regarding me with green eyes grown to the size of saucers. I don't know if I should be flattered or insulted, but the old expression "Peeping Tom" takes on a whole new dimension at times like this!

Last cow check was at eleven in a -20°F, crystal clear night. It made me think of a line from *The Cremation of Sam McGee*: ". . . the stars o'erhead were dancing heel and toe. . . ."

And so were the stars tonight, in a sky streaked with northern lights.

FEBRUARY 15

After a day of liveable temperatures (up to 20°F yesterday), we're back in deep winter. Light snow and a cold east wind all day. That meant mega-chores this afternoon. Then, as I finished feeding, I discovered that #88, a three-year-old due to have her second calf, wasn't eating but wandering around looking grumpy and unsettled. I stuffed her into the barn without much difficulty. Three hours later I came out for my pre-dark check and peeked into the barn. Sure enough, #88 had doubled! Now I had one big, solid cow and one little, wet bundle standing beside her. It was a good thing I had got her in. It will hit -20°F, still with snow and wind, tonight.

Before bed, I make one final check. In the barn, the new baby is lying stretched out on his side. Has he sucked? Is he getting chilled and weak? I walk over and start prodding him a little to see if he can get up. The next thing I know, #88, normally the mildest of cows, has her head down and is making a fairly earnest attempt to knock me over. Fortunately, the calf is between her and me so her reluctance to step on it, combined with the mighty roar I instinctively come out with when attacked, discourages her from giving me more than a little push. I go inside the stall gate and try reaching out from there to prod the calf. Then #88 gives the gate a good slam. I capitulate.

Either the calf is well or he isn't. One way or the other, his mother will have to deal with it herself. She is very definitely *in charge.*

FEBRUARY 16

A truly nasty morning. Between -15° and -20°F and snowing steadily. A good morning to sleep in but duty (spell that word c-o-w-s) called. I was out at seven-thirty checking for overnight calves—none, thank goodness—firing up the tank heater, plugging in the tractor and checking the calf in the barn. He was not only up and sucking but prancing a little as well. His mother had been absolutely right. She was looking after her child just fine without a nosy old bat like me sticking my nose in her business.

I came back in, made coffee and toast, picked it all up, along with the novel, and climbed back into my warm bed. I felt wonderfully pampered. If it wasn't for pitying all the critters out there in the cold (of which I will be one when chore time rolls around again), I could have a very nice day here in my cocoon.

FEBRUARY 17

It's one-thirty A.M. and -30°F outside, but for once I'm warm. Why? Because I've just spent the past forty-five minutes wrestling with a calf.

After having company until eleven-fifteen, I went out for a frigid, late-night check. As I shone the light around the sleeping herd, all seemed peaceful. Then I did a double-take. There, pale and ghostly with frost, stood a new calf. Yes, it was *standing.* The *mother* was lying down. Instantly, I rushed over, grabbed the poor little waif in my arms and headed for the barn. Unfortunately, I am not equipped with enough arms to carry a big, husky calf and aim the flashlight at the same time, so my next act consisted of tripping over a frozen cow pie and landing in a heap on top of the poor child. At last, calf and I staggered into the barn and I covered her with a blanket and then went back to bring her peacefully resting mother in. At least this cow was a totally placid type and wandered in without complaint.

Next, a run back up to the house for the hair dryer. Fifteen minutes of drying and massaging later, I tried unsuccessfully to get the calf on her feet again. Obviously, she was not strong enough to survive a night like this, even in the barn. So, I did something I'd never done before. With great difficulty, and absolutely no finesse, I loaded the calf in the back of the 4 X 4 and hauled her up to the house. As I write this, she's sleeping on an old horse blanket in front of the woodstove in the porch, sharing Timothy's "apartment." (Meanwhile, poor Timothy is crouched apprehensively in his bed staring at the calf as if she just landed from outer space.)

Morning (Real *morning, I mean):*

The calf died. After a night of little snatches of sleep here and there, I woke up feeling like I'd been dragged through a knothole, "hung over" and aching in every muscle. When I checked the calf she was still alive, barely, so I called Ken to bring his stomach tube in hopes a feed of warm milk might save her. But, no luck. The calf died about ten minutes before Ken got here.

So it goes. You win some, you lose some. I feel badly about this one, not so much about the financial loss as for the calf itself. It tried. Any critter born on a night like that and still able to get up on its own four legs deserves to live. The fault was mine. If I'd checked an hour earlier, she would have made it. Still, there's no use in recriminations. Just try to do better next time—and *especially* try not to fall on top of another one! The good news is that it's warming up again.

FEBRUARY 18

Chinook! Up to about 30°F. A cow I hadn't expected to calve so soon fooled me. In the warm afternoon sun she neatly and unobtrusively produced a nice, healthy calf.

The wild animals are doing well, too. A big herd of elk have taken such a liking to my neighbors' greenfeed bales that they've made a path as wide as a four-lane highway through the snow to the bales!

Farther along the road, I pass a young moose grazing as unconcernedly as a cow in a roadside field.

FEBRUARY 19

Woke up to a beautiful sunny morning with woodpeckers laughing and hammering in the trees.

My last walk out to check the cows at ten-thirty was into a powerful chinook wind and a temperature of 35 above.

FEBRUARY 20

A nice sunny day with one new calf waiting for me when I got home from school and another born before dark.

When I went out to check the cows at dawn all was peaceful, so Missy and I had time for a walk out to the road in the mild gray morning. From my gate, I could see a half mile down the road to my neighbors' place where half a dozen happy elk were ambling lazily across the road after a night's carousing in the bales!

Owls were hooting when I checked the cows at ten tonight.

FEBRUARY 21

Another nice day. When I checked the cows this morning, the #68 heifer was switching her tail and looking thoughtful so I stuck her in the small corral and phoned to ask Jim to check her while I was at school this morning, just in case.

When I got home at one-forty-five P.M. I rushed out to see what had happened. Yes! There was a calf. There were *two* calves! But neither of them belonged to #68. Meanwhile, *she* had given up tail-switching in favor of contented cud-chewing.

Today's calves, children of the chinook, were born bright-eyed and bushy-tailed, eager to be on their feet and after some milk. The kind of calves that make this business all worthwhile.

FEBRUARY 22

This morning when Missy and I went to check the cows she disappeared into the woods and came ripping back in a wild game of tag with *three* big, bushy-tailed coyotes. She wasn't the least bit worried, and they seemed to have no thoughts beyond a friendly romp with cousin domesticus, but I called her back and explained that three-to-one odds did call for caution!

No calves overnight, but an interesting phenomenon awaited me at noon. A newly calved cow was solicitously following a calf through the deep snow at the bottom end of the corral while another new calf lay twitching its ears and trying to get its bearings under a tree, also in the snow.

Twins! I thought. Omigosh! What do I do now?

Then I took a second look at the calf being pursued by the cow. He looked familiar somehow. He ought to have. He was #20's calf born yesterday.

I got #20's attention and persuaded her to entertain her own calf. Then I chased the other cow (#1) back to the calf under the tree. "Oh," said #1, somewhat embarrassed. "Where did you come from? You seem to be mine. How could I have been so careless as to misplace you?"

She commenced to mother him. I got him a forkful of straw to lie on, at which point he immediately stood up instead. Now he's been sucking for twenty minutes straight so I think the world is unfolding as it should, for a while.

I'm writing this on the boardwalk on the south side of the house, basking in the sun and listening to the water run down the drainpipes as snow melts off the roof. The chinook wind sighs through the trees and chickadees sing their spring song. It's 52°F in the shade.

FEBRUARY 23

Another nice day. Just as the sun went down tonight a jet raced across the western sky leaving behind a trail that turned a wonderful shade of platinum-pink in the sunset.

Later, as I drove north toward Sundre to supervise a junior-high dance, the huge plume of smoke from the week-old fire burning in the Sunpine mill's sawdust pile glowed eerily in the darkness ahead. It made me think of all the war stories I've read, of nights aglow with terror and destruction, and made me realize how very grateful we should be for the peaceful life we've been granted in this time and place.

Meanwhile, at home in the cow department, it was not a peaceful evening. My big old long-horned Hereford, one of the few horned cows I have left, is one of my favorites. To me she looks like a traditional cow *ought* to look. She minds her own business and raises an excellent calf every year, but she gets just a bit excited under pressure. (Such as the time when she got her horns stuck between the metal bars of a round bale feeder. I called my faithful neighbor Jim and we were all set to have a major rodeo holding her still while we sawed off a bar, but fortunately, in sheer desperation, she gave a particularly violent twist of her head that turned her horns just right and she escaped on her own.)

Tonight she was about to calve. I'd known it all afternoon as she eyed the gate, looking for a chance to get out into the woods, and took a great interest in everyone else's calves. By six o'clock, her water broke, but after that, she wandered casually off to have a drink and eat some hay. I put her in the small corral and, when there was still no visible action at seven, headed off on my trip to town.

At ten-thirty I was home again and immediately out to check the cow. Two front feet and the tip of a nose show as the cow strains a little. I can see the calf's tongue is lolling out of its mouth, a possible sign that it is in distress. Anyway, five hours is a long time for a big old cow like her to calve. Something must be wrong.

I call Ken, who has just nicely got to bed. He says he'll come. I get out the calf puller (which I haven't had to use for two years) and head back to the house for the traditional bucket of hot water. By the time I have performed the tricky feat of carrying the bucket of steaming water down the steep, ice-covered trail to the bridge in the dark, Ken is here. He has managed to chase the cow into the barn and given a little experimental pull on the calf's foreleg with the lariat rope. He thinks it moved a little but figures we'd better assemble the puller.

We're still standing in the doorway, looking at the cow, and trying to decide if we should rope her or put her in the smaller pen when, all of a sudden, the calf's head pops out. But the calf's not moving. I'm convinced it's dead. Then, the cow gives another push. Three quarters of the calf slips out. The cow continues to wander around the stall.

"It's alive!" Ken announces, rushing over to clear the membrane from its nose.

The cow gives one more push. The calf lands on the floor in a steaming heap. Ken continues to work on its nose. The cow turns around to see what's happening and discovers this person bothering her child. Head lowered, horns gleaming like scimitars, she starts toward him, murder on four hoofs. Simultaneously, I roar "HO COW!" from the doorway and step forward to distract her while Ken skitters (he's amazingly agile at times like this) around the corner and over the fence.

Pleased to have straightened up affairs so well, the cow kisses and nuzzles her baby, still glaring balefully at us for being here at all. Amazingly, the calf is perfectly healthy, alert and ready to get on with life. Ken goes home to have another try at a night's sleep. Gratefully, I also retire.

FEBRUARY 24

A mild day but hazy and damp until late afternoon when the sun shone through for an hour.

Just at supper time the #86 heifer finally decides to calve, a task she accomplishes in an hour with no commotion—are you listening, Longhorn? However, after two later trips to check on them, I can't decide if she's letting the calf suck or not. The calf is lively and eager but the heifer seems restless, refusing to stand still and once even kicking him gently away. I thought it was just my presence making her nervous so I shut them into the small pen in the barn to try to sort it out overnight.

The days are lengthening. Almost twelve hours of useable light today. Not yet quite dark at six-thirty tonight.

On my late check of the cattle the night was breathtakingly beautiful. No moon, but a million clear bright stars—and half the sky streaked with northern lights. The sky is one shade lighter than black and the dark spruce stand silhouetted against it, caressing the chinook wind as it sighs through their branches. The only other sound is the comfortable grinding of contented cows munching their way through their hay. On the way back to the house, Missy, the wonder cattle dog, pauses briefly to give a sleeping cow two swipes across the nose with a long, wet tongue. The cow bobs her head and snuffles disdainfully, too lazy to get up and run this presumptuous piece of fur out of her territory. Missy trots on, pleased to have done her own small bit toward perestroika.

FEBRUARY 25

An undecided day weatherwise. Mild and starting out sunny, but soon dulled by Sunpine smog in the air.

The heifer and her calf sorted out the sucking arrangement. Happily bonded, they rejoin the herd.

"Little Nasty" calved this morning. Her name is self-explanatory. "Little" because she's small, possibly due to a shot of Angus blood that's been in the herd from the days over twenty years ago when Dad and his friend Reuben Olson shared a grazing lease in the Nitche Valley. Reuben had black Angus cows. Dad, Herefords. Bulls of both breeds ran with the herds all summer. Usually one or two off-color calves showed up in both the herds each year—proof either that cows *aren't* racist or *are* color-blind!

The "Nasty" part of her name, she earned for herself. Jim and I pulled her first calf, after which she thanked us by running us out of the barn with murder in her eye.

Her second calf was born early one beautiful spring morning. When I went out to check the cattle it was up touring around as if it owned the place. Like a street urchin begging handouts, it was unsuccessfully hitting up every cow it saw for a suck. Why? Because its own mother was lying pathetically stretched out on her side and looking near death with her calf-bed pushed out in a big, revolting mess behind her.

I called the vet. By the time he and I got to the corral, Little Nasty was up, and not nearly as close to death as I had first assumed. Her first act was to run the vet up the fence.

The damage was repaired. (The damage to the cow, I mean. Fortunately, the vet sustained none.) And throughout the whole procedure, that wonderful, crazy little calf, who had obviously taken prenatal assertiveness training, just kept pushing in there, demanding a drink. At one point the mother fell on top of the calf but that inconvenience deterred the child only briefly.

I should have sold Little Nasty the following fall, but she seemed to be completely recovered. And I couldn't stop thinking about the amount of "try" that was born into her calf. A bloodline with that kind of courage should not be disposed of lightly. I kept the cow.

Last year, she calved uneventfully. This year, so far, so good. The calf is here. The cow has all her pieces in place. Another twenty-four hours, and I'll start to relax.

There are times when I find cows about as funny as an impacted wisdom tooth, but this morning as I look around, everything about them seems hilarious.

The heifer's new calf is the oddest looking little creature with hair curled so tight she looks like she's had a bad perm. When she was first born I was afraid something was wrong with her because her rows of curls were so tight that I could see the skin between them.

And there's old Longhorn who had to interrupt rooting in the greenfeed to rush over and guard her calf because the dog was passing by. She took off with one long stalk of oats draped artistically over each horn, making her look like some pagan goddess of the harvest.

And the latest addition, Little Nasty's child (another calf born with guts and determination), has already managed to struggle to his feet to stand with all four feet spread for the widest possible support base. He looks like a damp, brown-upholstered sawhorse with a head tacked on. Nasty gives him a couple of brisk swipes with her big tongue. He doesn't even stagger. Look out, world, this one's on his way.

FEBRUARY 26

A cooler, 20°F morning. Silhouetted against a pink and blue sunrise sky, a pileated woodpecker pounds out a tattoo on a dead snag. A faint kiss of warm breeze floats in from the west. Clear daylight by seven. (From here it will be a headlong rush to the longest day.)

All is calm among the cows. Little Nasty and her calf spent the night in the barn after she jangled my nerves a bit yesterday afternoon. She had managed a minor prolapse and seemed to be earnestly trying to push it into something major. With her history, I wasn't about to take chances, so I stuck her in the barn to keep her from lying down on a downhill slope and also so I could give her a big private pile of hay to keep her mind off pushing, and, last but certainly not least, so she could be more easily subdued if medical attention was required. The strategy worked. She's all back together this morning.

The day has grown complex since morning. Due to a special event the school timetable was rearranged, so I was to teach in the afternoon instead of my usual morning. No problem. I got the feeding done by midmorning and noticed, happily, that a cow was about to calve in the warm sunshine. Good timing. Go to it, cow.

Ten minutes before I had to leave, I ran out for a quick check on the cow. The calf should be born by now. But what to my horror-stricken eyes should appear but *one* calf foot, one *hind* foot! A backward calf is cause for concern. A backward calf with a foot curled back is cause for major panic. Human intervention is usually required. And here I was, all dressed for school, with ten minutes to work with. Time to yell for help.

I ran up to the house and phoned Marilyn. She said she and Ken would come right over and see what they could do. But I'd have to leave before they could get here. And there was the cow, still out in the middle of the big corral, behaving very calmly with just me around but likely to go plumb strange if anyone else showed up. At the very least I had to get her into the little corral. But the little corral was still occupied by Little Nasty and her calf. I rushed to evict them, beginning by trying to rouse the sleeping calf. Little Nasty took one look at me brazenly molesting her child and became more than a little nasty, making determined runs at me while I alternated between shinnying up the nearby fence and kicking her in the nose with my rubber boot. It's hard to say which one of us would have won two out of three falls but I didn't have time to find out. I left Nasty standing victoriously over the still-sleeping calf and went to chase the new client in. Mercifully, she was agreeable, particularly after I roared at her and waved the pitchfork. Into the corral she went. I'd decided it would be even better if she went into the barn.

But by this time she was over standing right beside Little Nasty, admiring her child and wondering if it wouldn't be easier to adopt than to deliver one of her own. Cautiously, I separated them, got the patient into the barn and raced off to school. On my way I met Marilyn and Ken on their way out.

An hour later I phoned Marilyn at her home number. She was there.

"So what happened?" I asked breathlessly, imagining all sorts of dreadful scenarios.

"Oh," Marilyn said calmly, "by the time we got there she'd had the calf. We looked in the barn door, saw that the calf was alive and moving, also saw the look the cow gave us and Ken said 'Oh, it's *her*. Let's get out of here and leave her alone.'" (*Her* went over the top of the squeeze gate when being ear-tagged as a yearling. Another year, it was wet and sloppy weather and she'd just calved in the corral when Marilyn and Ken came to visit so I got them to help me put her and the calf out into the pasture so they could bed down under the dry spruce. *Her* got so addle-pated then over being harassed by strangers that she instantly set off for the west end of the quarter, leaving her poor bewildered baby standing alone with his face hanging out. It took me all afternoon to get her to come back and collect him.)

So this time Ken did not get involved, especially since she had already solved her own problem anyway. (I don't know why Ken doesn't hang out his shingle as a vet. Just tell the cow he's coming and she cures herself. It's happened twice in four days!)

However, the Walkers' trip was not entirely wasted.

"I locked up the house for you," Marilyn says. "And, by the way, did you *mean* to leave your ice cream sitting out on the counter? I didn't think so, so I put it away for you."

Maybe the cow *didn't* need help but, obviously, *I* did.

When I check after school, *Her* is lying down beside her calf, chewing her cud and smiling. I think she's mellowing in middle age.

Another cow is on the prod, marching around, bawling, taking an interest in other cows' children. I'll bet . . .

I chase her into the corral. Twice, in fact. The first time, I close the gate but neglect to notice that I've left both front and back barn doors open to air it out. Minutes after I put the cow into the corral I look around to see her purposefully striding right through the barn and back to where I found her in the first place. Instant replay time.

At nine-thirty I go out to check on her and feel vindicated for my efforts. A bright and healthy calf is already at her side, up and sucking.

So ends another quiet day on the ranch!

FEBRUARY 27

A beautiful day with the intoxicating spring sun bathing the world. When I checked the cows at noon a new little stranger was just beginning to percolate on the warm straw. All the other cows and calves were fine, the calves either sleeping or taking little experimental jumps to figure out just how all those moving parts work.

I started to climb over the corral fence and came to a halt halfway, spending the next few minutes just sitting there, basking in the sun and the peace. It took a real argument with myself to get me moving again.

In the evening, I drove to Bowden (forty miles northeast) for a presentation at the public library. Afterward, all the way home I was beckoned westward by a huge lazy crescent moon, reclining on his back with the ghost of the rest of his circle cradled on his lap.

FEBRUARY 28

These "spring" days are almost too good to be true. A happy new calf was waiting for me first thing this morning, another arrived during the day and yet another in the evening.

It was shirt-sleeve warm today, so warm that things are getting a bit confused. While walking through the barnyard, I heard a miniature motor, looked and there was a *bee* buzzing around, happy as if he was in his right mind! Back to bed, bee. Don't push your luck. This day last year it went down to -25°F overnight.

March 1

The first month of spring, and we're still having spring weather. Another bee today, or maybe the same one again. It's hard to tell them apart when they all wear the same uniform.

The whisky jacks have suddenly started talking in sweet-tone twitters and burbles, entirely different from their usual call. This can mean only one thing: romance is in the air!

There was another sure sign of spring today. Morris, the ancient orange cat who has hugged the house with the zeal of a confirmed couch potato for four months, suddenly appeared in the farthest corner of the barnyard looking positively bright-eyed and bushy-tailed as he inspected the premises.

March 2

As Missy and I walk out in the early morning sun to check the cows, she suddenly stops and stares to the west. I follow her gaze and catch a glimpse of a long line of elk just 200 yards away, slipping majestically, single file, through the trees.

March 3

Another beautiful day. Marilyn and I walked up to check the horses. They're doing fine. Too fine. Even after a winter of rustling through deep snow for her groceries, Rainy is severely over-upholstered!

March 4

Two pileated woodpeckers making a big commotion, flying, hammering, giggling. Romance is in the air!

A pleasant surprise while checking the calves. A cow I hadn't even put in the big corral yet appeared with a nice, big bull calf in tow.

March 5

A morning of skies. In the north, a pileated woodpecker drumming high on a snag against a just-turning-blue dawn sky that is touched with little waves of apricot cloud. In the east are dark spruce silhouetted against the burning-gold sunrise.

At sunset, a big, tame raven sits on a post by the corral. Missy goes to run him off but, like a portly old gangster, he sits unperturbed, giving her a look that seems to say, "Nevermore, sweetheart."

March 6

Spring must truly be here! The sun rose so early that I missed the best part of the sunrise, but brilliant sunshine poured into the house by seven-forty-five. And, another sure sign of spring awakenings among the wild ones, a tang of skunk hangs over the hillside this morning.

March 7

The calves are feeling their oats these days. Two of them play king of the mountain, trying to push each other off a big mound of dirt. I've witnessed this same scene many times before, among kids during recess. Children are a lot the same, whatever their species.

March 8

A mysterious smoky morning. (Still Sunpine!) The sunrise is diffused to a gold-apricot glow. Two happy new surprises by their mothers in the barnyard. The Prince mousing from a fencepost by the creek.

The morning turned bright and sunny as I headed off to a teachers' convention in Calgary, so bright that, after a winter of driving the truck, I treated myself to the trip in my white Firebird GTA. The car is my only vice in an otherwise disgustingly sensible life. Lean, mean and fast, it's a pure pleasure to drive on dry pavement, and a pure nightmare on snow and ice. Which brings me to the day's adventure . . .

Sure enough, a typical Alberta lightning change of weather. By midafternoon a snowstorm blew in. Instantly, I lit out for home! All through the city I drove through a blizzard, barely able to see the other cars around me, and getting more scared by the minute. Visions of sliding sideways down the huge hill at Cochrane danced vividly through my head. I clutched the wheel in a death grip, glued my eyes to the road and forged on, like the legendary U.S. mail through snow, sleet, hail . . .

That seventy-mile trip seemed like a circumnavigation of the globe but, mercifully, I arrived home with the white bomb intact, and with a headache worthy of a whole week of teaching junior high. However, two aspirins and a cup of tea later I was sufficiently recovered to go out and check the cattle. Nature had enjoyed getting her jollies at my expense. Now the storm was over and she smiled benignly from a clear blue western sky, casting a silver glow over snow-dusted trees and billowing clouds that rolled away to the east.

The clean, fresh snow was interesting (much more so now than when I was wallowing through it in the car). The first layer was ordinary, but on top was a skiff of pellets instead of flakes. Just as I said, I really did forge through snow, sleet and hail.

Just at sunset, thirteen ravens fly west, crockling to each other. Is there some portent in this mystic number of mystic birds on this turbulent day?

No. Nevermore.

March 9

Enough snow has gone for me to make an after-supper exploration in the wild country just southwest of the yard. Missy and I nose around—I, because I'm looking at scrub brush I need to clear out to lighten up the yard a little, and Missy because she loves to nose around.

At six-thirty we come out of the woods in the gray twilight and look toward the house. It sits serene and at peace, little puffs of smoke coming from the chimney, a single lamp making a warm circle of light in the living room. It looks like home.

At ten I go out into a gentle night to check the cattle. The night seems still, yet it has its sounds. Sounds that seem soft and muffled by darkness. Far up in the woods, a cow bawls. A distant dog barks. A plane drones its way overhead. Closer, the sound of full-bellied cows, sighing and groaning pleasurably as they lie chewing their cuds. The creek, running freely on top of the winter's ice, gurgles and gulps.

All is well.

MARCH 10

On this warm spring day the cows packed up their children and moved up to the field, so I fed them up there.

At five-thirty I walk up there to see them. Pale golden light from the low sun back-lights the herd of grazing cows and sleeping calves, bathing them in a glow of well-being and contentment.

Later in the evening, I check on a cow I've been watching in the corral. Sure enough, just as the day fades into night and a full moon rises in the east, a calf is born. Her name should be Luna or Nocturne, something elegant and classical. But, I'll bet she'll just have to settle for being Ol' Brockle's Calf.

MARCH 11

Woke up to snow. Lots of it. Coming down in big, feathery flakes and turning the yard into one of those shake-up glass bubbles you can buy to make miniature snowstorms.

Since it looked like it might be planning a major storm, my first move was to let the four cows with calves that were still in the corral go out into the pasture to shelter in the spruce forest. Then I fed the outside cows, the inside cows, the bulls, put out some bedding, carried in some wood—and got soaking wet in the process. One perverse rule of this lifestyle is that you always end up spending more time outside in bad weather than in good.

MARCH 14

A cow really got my goat last night. (How's that for a magnificently mixed metaphor?) I was tired—I hadn't slept well the night before—and I knew I had to be up early for a trip to Red Deer in the morning, so I went to bed early. I drifted off to sleep by about ten-fifteen, only to drift back awake by eleven. A cow was bawling. No, make that *trumpeting*. She was at least 300 yards away, down the hill, across the creek and on the other side of the barn, but her dulcet tones came into my bedroom loud and clear. I buried my head and tried to coax sleep to return. I will not hear her. I will not hear her . . . AHMOO! I will *not* hear her. Blissful silence. She's stopped . . . AHMOO! Every two minutes. Sleep starts to sidle coyly away from me. It's no use. Now I'm listening for the next moo, so tense my toes are curling.

I get dressed, grab my trusty flashlight and forge out into the night to see what dreadful fate has befallen her calf. I stop to stick the dog in the granary. I do not need to be trampled by an irate mama charging *her* in the dark.

I track down the cow by following the AHMOOs. She sees me coming, strolls fifty feet and noses a sleeping calf. He gets up and begins to suck. The AHMOOs cease. Happiness has returned to the cow world. I stand there scratching my head in the moonlight, wondering what on earth that whole performance was about.

Oh well, it was a lovely night for a walk.

MARCH 15

I walked up to the field to look at the cows after supper, and found out why I don't feel the need to travel to exotic places. This is an exotic place.

The field is bathed in golden sun and dotted with contented cows and calves. Near the creek, a small, well-tailored owl perches in the top of a poplar tree, surrounded by dazzling blue sky. It reminds me of the line from Tennyson's "The Eagle:" "Ringed by the azure world he stands."

As I circle the tree, trying to get a better look at the owl, something else catches my eye. Just a couple of hundred yards away, an elk, make that a whole herd of elk, stand up high on the beaver dam, their hot breath making little clouds of steam against the sky. I walk slowly toward them. I'm more than halfway there before they make a move. Suddenly, with much crashing and crunching, they begin to leap away. I count at least a dozen. I stop walking and watch. They, too, stop, and stare back, unconcerned. I've seen cows that were wilder.

I come home. As I walk up the hill to the house, a woodpecker plays "Taps" to the setting sun.

MARCH 18

It's spring! How many snowstorms ago did I last make that same proclamation? But it must be real this time. The barnyard is becoming a muddy wallow, little streams race through the hayfields, the creek ice gives menacing creaks and groans when Missy runs across it, and everywhere is the sound of dripping water.

This evening I walk into the red room (so named because of its carpet and lack of a better name) and a drifting aroma instantly sweeps me back more than thirty years to the days when I visited in the tiny kitchen of my great aunt's house. It is the smell of heated cast iron given off by the ancient cookstove that once warmed her kitchen and now serves just as faithfully in this house. So many smells go along with a woodfire. Each kind of wood brings memories of different times and places. Freshly split dry spruce always diffuses Christmas into the air. The bark of long-dead poplar smells sharp and peppery like a high-country forest in autumn. All of them spell warmth and cosiness, a place to draw close to as darkness falls.

MARCH 19

A spur-of-the-moment trip to Banff (about two hours) today. The mountains were beautiful as always but the town of Banff, in March, was a bit of a disappointment. Caught between her glistening snow-cloak of winter and the green, flower-studded gown of summer, she looked like any other town in spring, grimy and gray. It was like visiting a great actress too early in the morning and catching her with her hair in curlers and without her make-up.

Tonight, when I let the dog out the sky is filled with stars. The sound of rushing water comes up from the creek.

MARCH 20

The great, slow wheel of the seasons grinds faithfully on. As Missy and I walk in the damp gray early morning, she stops at the little creek for a drink, just as she stopped on a late-October walk. That day, to her consternation, the water had gone solid on her. Today, to her delight, the water was wet again.

MARCH 24

Still cold. Not that unusual for this time of year but after all that nice weather last month a return to winter makes me feel cheated and very impatient for spring.

The calves are growing up. In the field today, I noticed Missy standing in the middle of a group of calves, actually touching noses with one, and not a single mama was having hysterics.

In the late-afternoon sun the beaver-dam ice creaks and groans menacingly. Both Missy and I turn to stare but there is no outward sign of breakup. It must be an internal injury, or just the ghost of winter past walking across the ice.

MARCH 25

A good spring sun today, but the wind is straight off an iceberg. Missy thinks it's warm, though. I came home from church to find her sprawled comfortably across the biggest snowbank in the yard, with a scoop of snow on the end of her nose for a garnish.

MARCH 28

After several days' imprisonment with night temperatures well below freezing, the creek is slowly breaking loose again. This morning, water trickled over the ice, catching the early sun and flooding the whole little valley with a wonderful light.

If variety is the spice of life, this is a spicy season. In the deep, shady, undisturbed places, the snow is still over my boots. In the sun, it's down to a rotting ice-crust. I purposely tromp on the crumbling edges of the ice patches, doing my share to hurry spring along. In the fields, streams and swamps of ice water glisten everywhere. In the trampled spots, the ground has turned to greasy mud, but on the sunny slopes, the earth is already almost warm and dry enough for a picnic.

The calves are becoming "teenagers," rude and boisterous now, bouncing up to the dog with heads fiercely lowered, trying to bluff her into running away. She ignores their mini-challenges just as she usually ignores their irate mothers.

March 29

With the shifting of seasons, the bird population also changes. This morning the treetops are full of the whistling and scrackling of nondescript brownish birds. The much-maligned starlings, no doubt. Personally, I have no particular quarrel with the starlings. I've never caught them at their dastardly deeds and I refuse to hate them on hearsay. After all, if I knew *everything* that some of my human acquaintances had ever done, I'd probably hate them, too—and they, me.

Coming home from an early-morning walk, I thought I heard a robin singing. I traced the sound to the very top of a huge bushy spruce but I still couldn't see a bird. Then, suddenly, he flew. As he winged eastward above me the sun set his underside ablaze with orange fire. Yes! A realio-trulio robin! The first one this year.

March 30

When I walked out into the woods this morning the pileated woodpecker was down on the ground chipping ants out of a rotten stump, wood flying in all directions from his mighty chiselling. He looked strange there on the ground, this big black and white bird with his long neck, fierce beak and brilliant red hat, somehow out of place in our conservative temperate (or should that be sub-arctic?) forest. He should have been deep in the Brazilian rain forest, or in a Dr. Seuss book or pounding away in a yuppie toy store with a lot of other expensive windup toys. But, none of those places can have him. He's *our* exotic bird and I'm honored to share this piece of earth with him.

March 31

A moist and misty west-coast day that began with spitting snow, a little rain, low-hanging clouds and ribbons of fog. It ended still gray but with the clouds promising to break and a robin in the very top of a big spruce serenading the lightening sky.

April 1

The world is alive with birds. Chickadees, filling the air with the clear, pure notes of their spring song. A white-breasted nuthatch, looking like a big chickadee, explores the yard, proving his nuthatchness by running headfirst down a tree trunk. In the woods, starlings whistle and grackle at each other. Across the road, in beaver dam country, there are loud geese conversations.

The first day of daylight saving time. From now on it will be hard to settle to inside jobs in the long, light evenings.

April 2

Last night The Prince stayed in and, daylight saving time and all, he got up and went out at five A.M., just exactly the same time he was going out *before* the time change. Who set *his* clock ahead?

Every time I go to town I pass a big, low-lying field. Its owners seem determined to make it the most perfect field in the world. They have worked it until the soil is like black flour. Last summer they didn't even plant a crop, just kept tilling and applying herbicide until, at last, not one green spear dared lift its head above the ground. Now, as the snow melts and the spring streams make their inexorable way downhill, they leave behind clear paths in that field. Tons of perfect, pure, black soil seep out to the ditches with the water, leaving broad gullies behind. I think I'd rather have put up with a few wild oats and a little quack grass if it would have saved the soil from being forever swept away.

Today I saw the season's first mosquito. The season's first mosquito also saw me. She lit delicately on my arm and prepared to drill. I then *killed* the season's first mosquito. Too bad. There's something *almost* lovable about these early-spring mosquitoes. They're so big, and awkward and slow—a cross between long-legged colts and massive army helicopters.

April 4

It snowed all day, a light, steady snow that melted on the roads as it fell but trimmed the trees with Christmas icing again. Alberta's version of the April shower.

The robins don't seem to mind this snow. Two of them sit on the soggy lawn, reefing out worms.

The creek is cutting down through the ice, etching an ice canyon almost three feet deep in places, winding through layer after layer of sculptured ice.

April 8

Well, after a couple of days of mixed cloud and sun, we're really into snow again. It started during the night and seems to be planning to continue all day. Several inches already and it's supposed to be well below freezing tonight and tomorrow so the snow will stick around for a while.

A disgusted robin sits stodgily under the umbrella of a big spruce on the lawn, no doubt considering suing the travel agent who sold him a ticket to an Alberta spring. I don't blame him.

One small blessing: two late-coming calves were born a couple of days ago, so they were well on their way before the storm hit.

April 9

The second week of April and right back in the belly of winter. Only 20°F this morning, with about six inches of new snow over at least six inches of mud, and still snowing a fine, middle-of-winter kind of snow. At times like this I can almost forget how much I love this country.

This evening, three fluffed-up juncoes sit disconsolately on the snow-clumped lilac, probably thinking, "Why we left our home in the south to roam round the Pole, God only knows!"

Cuddle up together, guys. It's going to be winter-cold tonight.

April 10

A real nothing morning! Literally. It's 0°F at seven-thirty with the sun rising in a blazing orange ball, trying to give at least the illusion of warmth. A chickadee sings his spring song over and over. Is he trying to call back the lost spirit of spring, or just to convince himself that there really is hope?

Twenty-nine elk banqueting cosily at the neighbors' bale stack, undeterred by the weather.

April 14

Spring creeps slowly but inexorably onward. The snow is almost gone. Quacking conversations again echo from the beaver dams across the road. High in the sky, a pair of hawks sails in lazy circles, riding the wind, while deep in the woods a ruffed grouse drums out his courting song.

The creek ice is wearing out. A thin, jagged layer, shaped like a shark's jaw, hangs high above the rushing water, slowly dripping itself into oblivion.

I dig in the flower bed tonight, much to the delight of The Prince who sits possessively in a clump of dry delphinium stems, snagging each one that I try to pull out with a lightning-fast paw. Are we having fun yet? Yes, we are—both of us.

April 16

A definite greenness is creeping across the warmest hillsides now. Almost overnight the grass will be tall and shaggy and the miracle of new green will turn into the job of lawn-mower pushing.

I drove up to the south quarter to see the horses. A bonus: I also saw four beautiful mule deer grazing on a sun-drenched hillside. Later I took my first walk of the spring to the beaver dams across the road. Missy led the way down the lane, carrying a treasure, the ragged carcass of her favorite old slipper, newly discovered with the melting of the snow.

The beaver-dam country is the same, yet subtly transformed by the passing of another season of ice and snow. The dams are like miniature ocean tidelands, always changing. New areas are flooded while in others the water level lowers, leaving behind rich and sticky mud flats to explore. A few ducks swim on the open water of a half-thawed dam. They take off with a quacking commotion when they hear us coming. On a dry and sheltered hillside we find a den dug in the warm earth among the spruce roots. Coyotes, I suppose. I ask Missy if she thinks that anyone is home, but she declines to crawl in and find out. We leave the coyotes in peace and head for the shelter of our own den before dark.

APRIL 17

I walked up to the high field this morning and caught the horses, bringing Angel and Copper home to ride and putting Rainy and Flame into the bush pasture. The hard days of winter are over. Now there will be plenty of grass outside the hayfields.

As I led the horses out through the field gate a movement caught my eye. There, tall, proud and unconcerned by our presence, a ruffed grouse perched on a log. Just waiting for us to get out of the way so he could get on with the drumming, I'll bet.

I rode Angel up to look at the cows tonight. It felt good to be on a horse again after "winter retirement." There's only one problem with these spring rides: the horses are shedding by the handful and I'm convinced that every hair they lose, I attract. Now *I'll* be shedding for the rest of the day.

As I write this at nine-fifteen, it's almost pitch-black outside but, even through the window, I can hear a robin still singing at the top of his voice. I open the door and discover that *two* robins are singing, one at each end of the yard. I wonder, is this a territorial dispute, or just an old-fashioned battle of the bands?

April 19

At eight o'clock I walk out through a woods full of sunshine and birdsong to feed the cows. They are scattered out across a half-mile of field, grazing peacefully. But as they hear the tractor start, heads come up, and a tide of white faces begins to move across the field. Calves come galloping, bright-eyed and bushy-tailed, fat old cows come waddling . . . Kind of sounds like the rats in the old Pied Piper story.

The new spring "bugs" are coming out. Yesterday I found a furry black caterpillar marching purposefully down the lane. Gently, I picked him up and let him walk across my hand. He was like a fuzzy black accordion in motion. The sound of a miniature polka should have echoed in his path.

This evening I cultivated the garden. It's early for that. Amazing how that spot lay under the snow just days ago and now it's dry enough to work. I stuck in a few pea, onion and lettuce seeds while I was at it. I think those things can survive a little frost.

As I worked in the garden, a mint-condition, mint-green bug flew past on wings of gauze. Too perfect for a mere bug!

April 20

The mountains seemed very close today, ramparts of blue and white standing firm against a surf of clouds rolling endlessly against them.

April 21

Cowboy time again. The day for vaccinating, castrating and dehorning calves. A lot of people brand the spring calves now, too, but I don't. Mainly because my dad never thought it was necessary and his system worked.

As a kid, I loved this job. Bringing in the cattle, cutting out the calves, roping and wrestling them made me feel like a big-time cowgirl, straight out of the Old West. Now, I guess I've gone soft, or grown up. It's a dirty job that makes me feel mean and cruel, but it's a necessary one. All the Walkers come to help, and the work goes quickly and smoothly. By evening the cattle are back in the field, the calves recovering in a warm sun and gentle breeze.

Copper did his first cow-work today, bringing the cattle out of the field. Not particularly demanding work, but he paid attention and cooperated. I switched to Angel for separating the cows and calves in the corral. She's an excellent corral horse because she doesn't get excited in tight places, though sometimes she should get *more* excited and move a little faster.

APRIL 22

Earth Day. Which this corner of the earth celebrated by taking a bath and then putting on her most beautiful dress.

The first warm spring showers came and went all day. Tiny little sun showers. The kind where you can stand in the sunshine and watch the rain pouring down fields away—and vice versa. The rain brings out the earth's perfume, rich, clean and full of the promise of another season of green.

The lilac leaves are beginning to unfold against the warm south side of the house.

As the day ends, the most perfect rainbow I've ever seen stretches across the east, each end touching a different farmyard, painting ordinary drab barns and corrals in psychedelic violets and greens.

APRIL 24

After another showery day and night, the morning dawns with golden sunshine. The grass is again a little greener, and the early warmth sends mist rising from the frosty ground. A bright new bull calf stands blinking in amazement at this exciting new world.

April 25

Today I mowed the strip of early grass along the south side of the house. Strange how we wait impatiently for five months to see that first green grass and then, instantly, we chop its head off!

The calves are galloping and jumping again, all recovered from their operations. If they were humans they'd be lying around feeling sorry for themselves for weeks. What makes animals so much more resilient than people? I think the answer is mental, not physical. The animal doesn't have the capacity to reason about his dire condition so he just plods on, making the best of things, and soon he's back to normal. When old Timothy, the cat, had to have a leg amputated, he came home from the vet's the next day, tried to walk normally, tipped over a couple of times, changed his walking system and carried on with his life. Not-so-dumb animals!

April 26

Woke to two or three inches of wet snow—and more falling fast. All this after activating the lawn mower? The blue jay redeclares winter and lights, squawking, on the windowsill to scrounge a little breakfast.

April 28

Still snowing. It's been flurrying on and off for two days now with an accumulation of six inches of snow over who-knows-how-much mud. It's warm enough that the roads stay bare and wet and hundreds of birds flock to these islands in the snow. Driving to town becomes a challenge in bird-dodging as flocks of crows, starlings and robins sweep into the air at the last possible second to avoid being hit. Yesterday a bluebird and I had a near-miss and today I had to come to a full stop twice to avoid running over an unidentified newcomer who insisted on hopping along ahead of me instead of flying off.

Off to the side assorted ducks and snipes delightedly probe for lunch in the soggy ditches.

MAY 5

To my complete disgust (I've always considered being sick to be a total waste of time), I got stuck in the hospital for six days for surgery.

I was afraid that spring would come without me and spent the better part of the last two days prowling around the hospital grounds taking in the air and planning my escape! Today I got away. And spring was at home waiting for me. I wouldn't have traded driving into the yard this afternoon for a trip to anywhere on earth.

A smiling sun is just unrolling tiny, perfect leaves from their tight winter packages. The breeze soars across the yard with a kiss of summer warmth and the smell of greenness on its breath. Michael Walker, who has been baby-sitting the house and the fur people, is out cutting the lawn. Speaking of the furs, all four of them are snoozing lazily in the sunshine. Now and then from across the pasture comes the rusty croak of a frog just tuning up for spring. My neighbor Jim who's been in charge of the cows, tells me they gave up coming for hay last Monday so there must be lots of fresh green grass sprouting in the fields.

This evening, we open the gate and Scruffy, the bull, is released from winter quarters in the corral. He sets off eagerly to find the cows. Another cycle of breeding, waiting, calving begins.

MAY 6

Still a little intoxicated with the freedom of being back home, I woke before seven into a world full of sunlight and couldn't wait to get out into it. Walking through the woods this morning was like being right in the middle of one of those Sounds of Nature tapes you can buy. Robins, chickadees, woodpeckers, starlings, all singing and chirping at the tops of their voices. From the direction of the beaver dam come the crashings and splashings of the colony hard at work.

But by nine o'clock, a cold wind brings in clouds and, by afternoon, there are snow showers.

The day ends as it began, with the sound of birds. After dark, I can hear a determined grouse still drumming and, from somewhere, a woodpecker laughing softly. The last sounds of the day.

Well, not quite. After that Missy barks half the night.

MAY 7

Another summer-winter day that starts off with sunshine and turns mean by afternoon. By evening, it's snowing seriously. A robin huddles on a fence rail, his red waistcoat ruffled by a snarling wind.

MAY 8

Four or five inches of snow to wake up to this morning. The cows decide that it's winter and insist on being fed again. By noon, the warm spring sun is out and the snow is disappearing.

MAY 12

A whole week of miserable, cold and stormy weather. The leaves that started bursting out joyfully a week ago are held in suspended animation. They look pale and unhappy, hugging themselves like bathing-suited children on a chilly day. I'm sure that, given half a chance, they would roll themselves back up in their blankets and wait for better days to come. The peas I planted more than three weeks ago are up, but they, too, look gloomy, hunched down like they're trying to pull their knickers up to cover their freezing ears!

MAY 15

Another cold, gray, damp morning. The Prince gave up waiting for better weather and went hunting anyway. He came in with his underwear very soggy from stalking through the grass.

May 16

Still the wet weather continues. I drive to Olds, a town of about 5,000 some twenty-five miles east of Sundre, for supper with a friend, passing through a succession of showers, sunshine, rainbows, clouds and more showers.

The definitive weather statement these days comes from a pair of handsome mallards who obviously have nested along the water-filled ditch just off the shoulder of the north road. Every time I drive by I see them happily waddling along the edge of the road, entirely satisfied with their soggy promenade.

May 17

A story that began last Saturday and kept me in suspense all week ended happily today.

From a whole corralful of waiting-to-calve cows in February, I was down to just one high-strung heifer in there—with another cow and calf to keep her company. It seemed like this heifer would *never* calve. Several times a day I went to look at her. Nothing. Then, I got up on a dismal, raining and snowing Saturday morning and went to check on her. There stood the cow and calf. But, the heifer was *gone*. This was impossible! I checked behind every bush in the corral, in places too small to shelter a rabbit, never mind a cow. I checked the fence. All intact. But the heifer was nowhere to be found. How could this be? Then, suddenly, I knew. It had happened once before a year or two ago. I checked the place where the creek ran under the fence. Sure enough. The bottom rail was coated with cow hair, rubbed off as the foxy brute had scooched down and edged out by walking *in* the creek until she was outside the fence.

Now, she was long gone and could be anywhere in a couple of hundred acres of thick brush. I tried tracking her. The trail circled and soon mixed hopelessly with dozens of other cow tracks. Only blind luck would find her and none of that came my way that day. I knew why she had disappeared. A cow about to calve instinctively seeks privacy, a safe spot to hide her child until it is strong enough to hold its own with the herd. I didn't really care *where* she had this calf, as long as the delivery was uncomplicated. But this was her first calf. What if something went wrong? Well, this was one of those times when there was no point worrying. Nature would take its course.

For five days, no heifer. I was beginning to accept the fact that she had died out there somewhere. Then, today, as I walked out through the woods, I caught a glimpse of a cow ahead of me, walking toward the field where the other cattle were. It looked like she had a very young calf with her . . .

Yes! Nature had indeed taken its course, very successfully. My wandering heifer had come home, and brought her fine, young son.

Driving out to the greenhouse in Bearberry, a few miles west of Sundre, this evening, I saw a sparrow hawk perched on a power line, a limp mouse dangling from his claws. All in one flash, I felt delight for the successful hunter and regret for the unfortunate mouse. Almost every aspect of life is like that. It's a sweet wind that blows no one sorrow!

May 19

For variety, instead of just an ordinary shower, we have a thundershower, and a little soft hail thrown in for good measure. All the animals cosy into the house, especially Missy who is so scared of thunder that she practically climbs into my arms at even a distant rumble. No, Missy, it won't work. Whatever your dubious breeding may be, a lap dog you definitely aren't!

May 20

At last, a perfect sunny spring morning. As I sit on the deck, reading and drinking coffee, I am surrounded by birdsong. Suddenly, Missy and I both prick up our ears as a snatch of *human* song drifts in from the road. It's Jim, my neighbor, out for his morning walk, singing to himself, his warm, mellow voice fitting in perfectly with the other voices of spring. Missy trots off purposefully, no doubt on her way to give Jim wet-nosed greetings and to exchange dog-confidences with Jim's old black Lady dog.

This evening, after the season's first wiener roast, Marilyn, Ken and I walk up to the beaver dam. Along the way, white-breasted nuthatches are doing acrobatics on a poplar trunk. On the dam, two huge Canada geese float with the massive serenity of cruise ships. Even the busybody beaver who swims in circles around them, slapping his tail, doesn't so much as ruffle a feather.

May 23

A walk around the bottom of the back yard leads to an intriguing discovery. A huge old spruce is obviously ant-infested. It's half dead and leaking sawdust all around its roots. A closer inspection shows a skin-crawling sight that would fit right into an Indiana Jones movie.

In a depression in the tree's bark, there appears to be a dark, sticky stain, the size of your hand. But the stain is alive. It's a solid, squirming mass of bright and shiny, newly hatched winged ants. I'm not an ant expert but I wonder if these could all be young queens about to fly away and start their own colonies. Fascinating, in an itchy sort of way.

May 24

The ants have flown! Only a few wingless plebians remained on the tree today.

A distinctive birdsong led me out the southwest corner of the yard to stare into a poplar top until I finally spotted the singer. The rose-breasted grosbeak. I knew it would be him. He, and his ancestors before him, have been coming to that spot for fifteen or twenty years. In formal black jacket, white shirt and crimson bow tie, he's one of our most beautiful birds. His singing is beautiful, too. The only way I can describe it is like a robin's, but even better.

While looking for the grosbeak I came upon two other wonderful things I've never noticed before: morel mushrooms with their intricately etched caps, and the delicate, salmon-ink flowers of the wild currant bush. Strange how often you can prowl a patch of woods and still find surprises. Speaking of surprises . . .

The Apron cow, whose name has stayed off my police blotter for several months, has not gone straight after all. Bright and early this morning she was happily grazing in the garden.

May 25

More monsoons! About an inch of rain overnight, with a prologue of showers yesterday and an epilogue of showers today. Everything has taken on a Pacific Coast greenness. The creek runs high and muddy.

Maybe there is *one* advantage to this month of exceptionally cool and rainy weather. While often there seems to be a headlong rush from winter drab to full-blown summer, this time the leaves seem to be unfolding in slow motion. Their "Nature's first green is gold" stage that Robert Frost wrote about has lasted a whole month this year. Even now, at the end of May, the sweet and sticky balsam poplars are just unrolling their baby leaves, filling the air with a fragrance more wonderful than Chanel # Anything. Underfoot, too, the plants are in a kind of suspended animation, still tiny, newborn, and perfect—even the weeds.

May 27

The morning dawns bright and sunny. A few hours to enjoy the sparkling clean and green world before the floating clouds mass for the next onslaught.

Last night's sleep was a disrupted one—all due to The Prince and my imagination. I was lying cosily in bed, reading, at about eleven when, from outside somewhere, I thought I heard the shriek of a very disturbed cat. Morris and Tim were asleep in the house, so that left The Prince . . .

I got up and went to the door. Missy was on the rug just inside. She's had so many coyote concerts lately that I've been letting her sleep inside so I can get some sleep, too. But she wasn't sleeping now. She was standing up, all a-twitter, telling me that she, too, had heard something out there. I opened the door and she shot out and around the back of the house, barking. I started calling The Prince. No answer. I put on my rubber boots and my ski jacket over my nightshirt, grabbed a flashlight and began a trek around the yard futilely calling "Here Princey! He-e-e-re Princey!" No immense, elegant tail appeared, pointing skyward. No answering cat voice came out of the gloom. The Prince had been eaten in one gulp. Already there was a big hole in my life.

Resignedly, I went back to bed. But ten minutes later I was back on the porch calling. No Prince. Sadly, back to bed. This procedure repeated itself three or four times. Finally, Missy, who has to move off her rug for every one of my trips out the door, follows me out, puts her nose to the ground, resolutely trots off around the west side of the house and disappears into the darkness. I get cold waiting for her to come back and go back to bed.

Soon I'm up again, looking for the dog this time. She's nowhere in sight but what to my wondering eyes does appear but The Happy Prince, swaggering up the steps, all flags flying, not looking the least bit like a cat who's been eaten in one gulp.

I welcome him in, soggy underwear and all. A minute later Missy appears on the porch, looking self-satisfied. Is it possible that she figured out that the only way any of us would ever get any sleep would be for her to go find that wretched cat and send him home to mama?

Speaking of the wretched cat, he immediately jumps onto my bed and begins the task of grooming the sticky tree buds, leaves, and rose bushes from his damp fur. Naturally, I tolerate all this. After all, he has just returned to me from the dead, has he not?

Having done a thorough grooming on the bedspread, and transformed himself into a soft, delightful, cuddly ball of fluff with whom one would gladly share a bed, The Prince then declines to sleep with me at all, preferring the privacy of a quiet corner under a chair. Until dawn, that is. Then, he wakes me up and announces that he has much important business outside.

Why do I get the feeling that wretched cat had a more rewarding night than I did?

The first hummingbird of the season dropped by—hovered by, that is—today. He checked all along the eaves, took a sniff at the flowering plum and then left. Consumed with guilt at my negligence in not preparing sooner, I rushed to fill and hang the hummingbird feeder. Sure enough, he did come back, made two more trips, took a couple of sips and then flew away.

MAY 28

Another day of showers. Just before dark I sit on the bench on the boardwalk for five minutes, breathing in the evening. It smells of soil and wet green grass. Missy jumps up on the bench beside me, adding damp dog to the spectrum of aromas. Several mosquitoes go to work on my exposed extremities. Time to go inside.

MAY 29

I sit sleepily over morning coffee looking out through a frame of glorious pink flowering plum outside the kitchen window. What I see beyond the plum is another damp gray morning and, centered in the picture, The Prince. He is seated majestically atop my white car, washing his muddy feet. Oh well, so what if I won't be able to see through the paw marks on the sun roof. There isn't any sun to see today, anyway.

MAY 30

Lovely weather for ducks. But, believe it or not, even the ducks seem to be getting waterlogged . . .

This evening as I crossed the bridge over the swollen creek, I noticed a water bird bobbing on the current just upstream. He was a handsome black and white bird. At first I thought he might be a loon. On second thought, I declared him to be a duck and the bird book confirmed him as a goldeneye. But what was he doing down here? Ducks don't live on this stretch of the creek.

I went on about my business, came back in a few minutes and found Le Duck resting on a mudbar in midstream.

A third trip found him back in the water, paddling energetically upstream and around the bend where the water goes under the fence. That was where he ran into trouble. Just through the fence was a turbulent spot where the water surged around a willow root. As he reached that spot, the current swept him backward, in spite of his best efforts. Two or three times he tried, before letting himself be pushed into a quiet backwater where he sat resting and treading water.

How did Le Duck get himself into this predicament? Why didn't he just *fly* upstream? Maybe a duck can't take off on fast-flowing water. There must have been some reason for his dogged pursuit of the water route.

Just before dark I went out one more time to see how he was doing. He was gone. I will assume that he made it through the rapids and on to smoother sailing.

Good luck, Duck!

JUNE 1

No, the end of the wettest May I can remember did *not* change the weather. Yesterday there was no rain, but today the June rains began with a thundershower that grumbled in about five A.M. and continued with heavy rain for most of the day. By evening the creek had overflowed into the bottom of the horse pasture.

JUNE 2

Flood! Rivers all over southwestern Alberta are running over and the ones around here are no exception. The most dramatic is the Fallen Timber, officially the Fallen Timber Creek but actually it's a gentle little river. Usually it's gentle. Today it's a monster, rampaging out of control, filling its valley with muddy, frothing water, flooding pastures and campgrounds, kidnapping picnic tables and carrying them away in its white-capped teeth . . .

At home, aside from the usual water in the basement, all is calm. The creek, which never did reach the real flood stage, is already subsiding. Fortunately the big beaver dam held. Otherwise, I might be writing this from my oceanfront property right here in sunny Alberta!

A long walk in the south woods is a journey into a dense green rain forest where every other step is a splash. Delicate woods flowers are coming out. A purple virgin's bower (blue clematis) climbs a spruce, winding a vine trimmed with beautiful, bell-shaped blue-violet flowers around the tree trunk. Under the trees, patches of purple-veined white wood violets bloom.

JUNE 3

A day without rain! That called for immediate action. Time to get the cows and saddle horses out of the hayfields again and give the hay a chance to grow.

Horses first. I walked the half mile to the north field with two halters. With two horses caught, the other two will follow. Well, usually they follow. This time they were having a visit with the neighbors' horses across the fence and refused to budge. Oh well. Later . . .

Having at least captured one horse, Flame, I saddled up and went to chase the cattle out. But the cattle didn't want out. They stood in difficult places and sulked. Almost every place was difficult. Those low-lying fields had turned into the Okeefenokee Swamp. Squish, splash, slurp, went the horse's hoofs. Mud landed here and there, on my clothes, my saddle, my hair.

I worked the cattle down to the gate, and discovered that a bunch were missing. It figured. The rest were across a deep, muddy draw in another field. The draw was so soft that I got off and led Flame across, no easy task when you're trying not to get yourself bogged down while watching out for a horse that may panic and decide to jump across the bog, carelessly landing on *you* in the process.

At last I get all the cows out of the field, only to see one old girl come busily trekking back in again, mooing worriedly for a calf she thinks she's forgotten. She makes a circuit of the field and goes back out, still without a calf, still mooing. Later, on the south quarter I see her happily grazing with the other cattle *and* her calf. What this little abberation was about, I'll never know.

Now, to get the other two horses. I catch Angel first, and lead her behind Flame. This goes badly. Apparently Angel does not like Flame. She spends her time sneaking up close behind, ears flattened, teeth bared, attempting to take a bite out of Flame's hindquarters. Not surprisingly, this makes Flame somewhat insecure and our progress is erratic. Furthermore, I have another problem. Now, *Rainy* refuses to follow. She's still at the fence, talking to the neighbors' horses. I try a switch, turning Angel loose and catching Rainy. Halfway across the field with Rainy, I see that *Angel* isn't coming. Now, *she's* visiting with the neighbors! I give up and make two trips.

Getting these animals out of the field has burned up half of my afternoon, and all of my patience! I did see a lot of wildlife, though—five thousand frogs.

JUNE 4

Back to rain. It's chilly tonight. Cool enough for Timothy and The Prince to curl up together peacefully in the big chair by the fire. That's *cool.*

Saw the first dragonfly of the year today. I hope he brings reinforcements. With this wet-weather mosquito crop, he's going to need all the help he can get!

JUNE 7

Still no settled weather! After one fairly dry day I woke in the early-morning hours to the sound of pouring rain again. It pelted down another three-quarters of an inch before, suddenly, at noon, a strange light appeared above us. It was the sun! The afternoon was bright and beautiful and I managed to put out a few more bedding-out plants. But of course the morning's rain made it impossible to make a foray into Dandelionville with the lawn mower. I've never seen the yard in quite such a mess. The lower part, which maintains its golf-course greenness throughout the driest summers, is now so wet that even walking across it leaves a trail of muddy tracks.

The wet weather is getting past being an inconvenience. Some farmers who were counting on getting grain planted are already out of luck. It's time that the green feed was in, but that's out of the question until we have several hot, dry days.

The birds are happy, though. Robins with beaks overflowing with soggy worms hop merrily across the rice-paddy mud-flats of the garden. Last night the woods rang with their singing. In the trees above me, white-breasted nuthatches and a hairy woodpecker are busily harvesting bugs.

JUNE 8

A full day without rain. I spent most of it outside, putting out the last of the bedding-out plants and managing to encroach with the mower a little farther into the tall-grass country of the lower lawn. The grass was so tall I had a whole wheelbarrowful of "hay" to haul away. Maybe I should have held onto it. If this wet weather goes on through haying season we'll need every wheelbarrowful we can get.

A reward of the wet spring is a patch of miniature white and pale green orchids growing right in the yard. Pale coral-root, the plant book calls them.

Missy has been leading a rather nefarious social life lately. For a couple of days she's been giving off mild emanations of eau de la skunk and this morning she greeted me with a single porcupine quill sticking out of her soft, black nose. At least she seems to be tempering her disasters with moderation these days!

JUNE 9

It's ten-fifteen and still daylight. Robins are singing in all directions. I see that the robins already have adolescent children from their first hatch. I startled a young one while I was out riding today. He made a good horizontal flight but lacked a bit in altitude—about three feet off the ground was the best he achieved.

This evening, as Missy and I walked along the lane, a grouse stood in front of us pretending to be invisible. He didn't move until we were about fifteen feet away, then hurried away on foot. I guess we didn't look dangerous enough to warrant all the bother of a takeoff. I took Rainy, my big buckskin, for a ride tonight, the first in a couple of years as, between a wire cut and another mysterious lameness, she's been out of commission. I enjoy the feeling of power and command that comes from riding a really big horse but I do wish that Rainy's withers wouldn't get lost in her ample upholstery. Too often I feel like it's only pure will power on my behalf that keeps the saddle from sliding around her smooth roundness and giving me a whole new perspective on the world from under her belly.

JUNE 10

A thunderstorm at five A.M. rang in the day. I looked out and found the fur family huddled worriedly on the step. (It had been such a nice night that I'd encouraged the whole gang to camp out.) Now, I invited them all in, including The Prince, who, not surprisingly, brought his wet underwear to launder on my bed. We all went back to sleep till nine.

It stayed gray and damp all day, but Missy and I went for a walk in the evening through a field of tiny purple violets and wild strawberry blossoms. But the walk was spoiled by a coyote's bedraggled carcass lying in the ditch, probably a victim of some well-meaning poisoner who thinks there are too many coyotes in the country. Maybe there are. But there are too many people in the world, too. And no individual, human or animal, wants to be sacrificed to balance the books. Anyway, I don't believe in poison for any reason. A dog poisoner terrorized Sundre this spring, destroying as many as twenty dogs and breaking at least that many hearts in the process.

JUNE 11

It's *just* pouring outside and I'm right out of cheerfulness. The only thing different about this rain is that it is freezing cold. The last couple of rains have been almost sub-tropical. In fact, last night there were tornado watches northeast of here. Fortunately, nothing significant developed.

But this feels like an end-of-September rain, and there is a forecast of possible snow in the foothills, which usually means here. The May snowstorm is a tradition but, in the middle of June? Too depressing to discuss.

As evening falls, a nasty day turns into a thoroughly nasty night.

It's not raining, or snowing, now, but the trees toss in a restless wind and fresh, green leaves occasionally float to the ground. A big, dead poplar in the horse pasture has blown down.

The only bright spot is the intrepid hummingbird who makes several trips to the feeder. How does that little scrap of feathers keep from blowing away like dust in the wind?

JUNE 14

A gold and blue day without a drop of rain! I rush around, madly cutting grass, and succeed in leaving muddy lawn mower tracks across the lower lawn. I knew better than to try the lowest part. It would have eaten the lawn mower as surely as the La Brea Tar Pits once sucked in ancient animals.

When I went to bring the dry bedding off the clothesline I met a pure white spider marching across a sheet, packing the half-drained corpse of a fly over her shoulder. I don't know where she was going but it took quite a tussle to get her off my laundry!

Tonight, coming home from a birthday party at ten-thirty, I drove into a beautiful orange and purple sunset. It was just dark enough to turn the car lights on.

JUNE 15

A few thunderclouds grumbled past but this is the *third* day in a row without rain!

I rode Flame up to the south quarter to see the cows. Everything is wet. What I always call the high trail is half under water!

I haven't ridden Flame much for a couple of years (she grass founders and gets sore feet by midsummer if I don't keep her on a strict diet), so I'd kind of forgotten her idiosyncrasies. She's half American saddlebred and, though she's a good cow horse, her eastern blood does show up in one way. She's a natural jumper. Not a Spruce Meadows-type jumper, she just tends to sail over obstacles that long-legged Rainy would climb over and practical Angel would go around.

I was reminded quite spectacularly of this jumping habit today. We were loping down a trail when, suddenly, we came upon a shallow puddle, about six feet across. I expected her to splash right through. I was wrong. All of a sudden, I felt her gather herself for a leap. Oh, no. I wasn't ready for this. I was leaning back when I should have been forward, pulling her in when I should have been letting her have her head . . .

Our jump was not a pretty sight. But when we returned to earth and I found myself still in, not behind, the saddle, I was more than pleased!

The lilacs are out, filling the air with sweetness. I always feel a little cheated when reading my favorite Wilbur Smith African novels that we don't have frangipangi and bougainvillea and all those wonderful-sounding flowers he writes about. But today we do have lilacs.

I brought a few in to perfume the house. I hope some lilac fragrance will evict the lingering odor of "eau de basement" left over from all our monsoons.

JUNE 16

Another beautiful, sunny day. I was cutting some grass in the evening and thinking I should go for a ride—if getting a horse across the creek from the pasture to the barn wasn't so much trouble—when Dale, a neighbor who pastures his cattle in Jim Haug's place, drove in with interesting news. My two bulls were in his pasture. Well, now I had enough motivation to go and get that horse!

I took Angel and headed for the next quarter north of me. Jim and Dale had found the hole in the fence and were fixing it, so I went after the bulls. Halvor was easy. I think he'd already lost in a scuffle with Scruffy because he was standing, panting, near the fence and quite willing to come home. Scruffy, however, was a different story.

I had to chase him through several dozen swamps. (Is there anything that's *not* a swamp this year? I'm sure it's the wettest spring in at least thirty years.)

Finally, I got Scruffy cut out of Dale's herd and started him toward home. Then, halfway across the pasture, he turned stubborn, doing a very good imitation of a muskox fighting off wolves by standing his ground, pivoting to keep his head always toward Angel and me. I doubt that he would actually have charged us, but there was no way he planned to run, either. Standoff.

Then, all of a sudden, in her first-ever right move with cattle, Missy jumped up and nipped ol' Scruff right on his big, wet nose. Instantly he forgot his belligerence and headed straight for home.

Now, he and Halvor are in the corral, thoroughly disgusted with the world and roaring at each other in tones more bearlike than bovine.

Shut up guys, and let us all get some sleep.

JUNE 17

It doesn't seem possible that nine months have passed since the fall roundup in September but here it is, cow-moving day again. Time to take them back to the north quarter for three months of summer pasture.

The first job is to get them out of the south quarter and into the corral at home to make sure nobody's missing. The thick brush and soggy ground in the south woods make this seem more like a safari into a rain forest than a roundup. After an hour or so of getting slapped in the face by passing branches, having my knees reduced in diameter by tree trunks that refuse to move over and getting well-splattered with the mud from a hundred bogs, I finally chase the last cow into the corral and close the gate. (This last action almost ends with me leaving both my rubber boots behind to propitiate the mud god of the gateway where the wet ground has been churned into gluey goo by some 280 hoofs.)

When I count, I *do* seem to have all the cattle. Amazing! Especially so since I chased them out of the thick brush mainly by homing in on the sounds of their crashing and splashing and hardly saw a cow till I got back to the corral.

At last the show is on the road, the herd moving out behind Walkers' truck with Marilyn and Ken going ahead to run interference, closing neighbors' gates, watching intersections, slowing traffic coming over the hill. I bring up the rear, riding Rainy now. None of the horses have shoes yet this year, so I use the hard-hoofed buckskin when I can't avoid riding on the gravel road. I don't chase cattle in the brush with her if I can help it, though. She's just too big. Over sixteen hands of well-upholstered frame just doesn't fit on a narrow cow trail with over-hanging branches, especially when there's a hapless rider to squeeze in, too. And, to make matters worse, being jammed into a small space makes Rainy nervous. The narrower the trail, the faster she goes! Other horses may be Jeeps but she thinks she's a Cadillac.

The road trip is uneventful. The cows move out eagerly. Then, we're at the pasture. A stream of sleek, red and white bodies pours in through the gate, flowing out into a sea of deep green grass, their slick hides gleaming with health under the bright Alberta sun. I watch with pride and satisfaction. This is what the cattle business is all about. Fat cattle on lush pasture. How dim and far away this scene seemed on those 40-below February days.

Suddenly, thunder grumbles off to the west, jerking me back to reality. We may be out of the snow season but rain is a definite possibility. Rainy and I set off for home at a spanking trot that soon turns into a ground-eating lope. Less than an hour after the cattle left home I'm pulling off the saddle and offering my horse the traditional bite of oats. I sigh with relief. Barring unforeseen difficulties the cows and I are on vacation from each other till September.

JUNE 19

A warm, sunny day. Right after school I take Copper out for a run, his first in nearly two months. He behaves tolerably well but could use a lot more polish.

After the ride I work on the garden and yard. While pulling weeds, I hear The Prince's voice, taking soundings as he prowls through the high grass along the garden. I look up. No cat. Only a tall black periscope of tail cutting a swath through the grass, just its bent tip glides along above the "waterline."

The chokecherry bush in the yard is in bloom, covered with bunches of fragrant white flowers. Every time I pass close by with the lawn mower a branch slaps me in the face. But at least it's a sweet slap!

As I write this, it's ten-forty P.M. The green of the trees is just beginning to fade to gray as darkness creeps in. Loud, cheerful robin voices break the evening stillness.

JUNE 22

After heavy showers yesterday, today was a perfect summer day. A ruby-throated hummingbird stopped by for a big drink and a tiger swallowtail butterfly sipped from the lilacs outside the window. A perfect picture, pale yellow wings against deep mauve flowers. All things bright and beautiful . . .

But in all fairness, I must admit that yesterday I saw two swallowtails sipping just as happily from a manure-rich barnyard puddle!

Back to the finer things. The chokecherry is absolutely abuzz with honeybees today. I'd like to follow them home and claim a share of their honey if it tastes as sweet as the blossoms smell.

The grass flowers (officially, blue-eyed grass) are in bloom. For some reason they are among my earliest childhood flower memories. A plant that really does just look like another blade of grass, until, suddenly, out burst beautiful little flower faces: five sharp-pointed, gentian blue petals, around a yellow center.

I sat down on the swing in the campsite at the bottom corner of the yard, and who should go scuttling away under my feet but the biggest toad I've ever seen. Very handsome, as toads go, and with enough capacity to eat every mosquito in the country. I wish he'd get started soon.

JUNE 23

As I come up the steps to the house, I meet a pair of ants going down. Successful scavengers, they're dragging the carcass of a worm bigger than the two of them put together. They reach the edge of a step, and carry right on down the vertical expanse of concrete. It's like watching two humans carry a motorcycle down the sheer side of Yosemite's El Capitan.

JUNE 24

As I write this at ten-fifteen P.M., the big spruces outside my bedroom window are just shading from green to black and an apricot-gold sunset glows between their branches.

Today was the Sundre Rodeo. I wonder how old I was when I went to my first Sundre Rodeo. I can't remember but I'm sure my dad and I went to at least twenty together. It was always a special time for me. I guess that I can identify with the song title "My Heroes Have Always Been Cowboys." The rodeo always made me feel close to a great, western tradition.

The earliest ones I can remember were in a little makeshift arena at the bottom of Snake Hill. The grand finale I will always remember came at dusk when a wagon train pulled into the arena, circled and unhitched. Then, suddenly, on the brow of the big hill, a line of riders appeared. "Indians"! With spine-chilling whoops they charged down the steep side of the hill, shooting into the air. (Were they shooting blanks? Who cares. Nobody got killed.)

A couple of circuits around the arena and then one of them touches a torch to the paper canvas of one of the wagons and it bursts into flames.

The flames die down and night falls. The rodeo ends for another year.

Great stuff, when you're a kid. Now, I'm sure it couldn't happen. Someone would cry "racism" and a protest would break out. Rightly so, maybe, but I think those were more innocent times. No one was making a statement that Indians were savages. Nobody was making a statement at all. It was just fun.

I probably drank some of my first coffee at the rodeo. Strong, black and hot from a cardboard cup as we shivered after a sudden downpour.

I remember another downpour at the rodeo, years later when the grounds had been moved to the far end of town and I was old enough to be racing Goldie, my one-in-a-million-bought-for-one-hundred-and-sixty-dollars horse in the stock horse race. I was out warming her up when the rain hit and I remember my round-braided rawhide reins, soaking wet, stretchy and slippery, making it almost impossible to hold back the excited horse until the starting gun. There was a lot of motivation to win that day. Only the front-runner finished with a clean face!

The grounds have moved again, back almost to the first site. The rodeo is professional now. The Gary Logan Professional Rodeo, named in honor of a local cowboy who died with three others in a plane crash in California a few years back. I sit in the stands and watch this year. The performance runs smoothly. High-class riders, good stock, a huge metal grandstand. The Sundre Rodeo has come a long way.

But I miss the wagon train, I miss the thrill of that grown-up coffee. I miss the adrenalin high of racing around a dirt track on a horse that loved to win. And I miss my dad.

JUNE 25

It's finally here. The time of year that makes staying alive through an Alberta winter worthwhile. If I had to define heaven, it would be "the way my yard is right now."

The air, sweet with lilac-smell, is warm with sunshine yet cool with a soft breeze. In the flower beds, perennials that have been watered like never before in their lives have shot up strong and tall. A battalion of oriental poppies stand tall and proud, their blaze-orange tunics glowing against the green grass. Ladylike royal purple irises wave their flags and exude a delicate scent. Columbines, both deep-purple and pink-mauve, welcome bees to drink from their bell-shaped flowers. The chokecherry is nearly finished blooming, but now beside it the red osier dogwood and mountain ash open their clusters of white flowers. Chives and rockets bloom together in almost identical shades of mauve while the gnarled old honeysuckle spreads over them its branches filled with swelling pink buds. Entwined with the mountain ash, a huge wild rose bush grows uninvited. For years I struggled to root it out but it held on valiantly until, at last, in spite of persecution it managed to put out one pure pink flower and shame me into letting it live. Now it is loaded with bursting buds.

And of course there are the pansies, crowds of purple and gold people with smiling faces upturned in greeting. (My friend Ruth always threatens to sing when she sees those expectant faces all obviously anticipating some great performance.) I admire the pansies above all other flowers. They start blooming with April snow still on their shoulders and are still blooming when November snow covers their faces. They'll grow in any soil, including the gravel of the driveway, and never need reseeding. The patch here was started twenty years ago and without a handout from anybody has prospered ever since. How did "pansy" ever get to be a synonym for sissy?

Early this morning Missy and I took a stroll out to the road. The bright sunshine glistened on dozens of dew-covered webs that were scattered around on the grass, each about as big around as a teacup and not the usual precision-built spider web. These were several layers of "silk" deep and appeared to have a haphazard plan, threads leading off in all directions rather than geometrically arranged. Who made these webs? What were they to catch? (So far, dandelion seeds appear to be the only prey captured.) Did minute Martians land and leave these traps behind? Or were they spun by a spider who had just eaten a fermented fly and was having trouble spinning a straight line? Alas, I'm afraid we'll never know.

The rufous hummingbird was here tonight, a spectacular red fellow who arrived with a whistle and whir of wings, sampled from the feeder, flew to the very top of a spruce and perched for a long time before coming to sip some more.

JUNE 29

Emancipation Day! School is over. The pace suddenly changes. Fewer deadlines. Life runs less by the clock, more by the weather—and by whim. (I was out cutting grass in my housecoat and rubber boots at nine-thirty tonight. Who needs a logical reason for that?)

Images of the day:

A red-winged blackbird perched on a power line, his scarlet epaulets flashing against a blue sky.

A big fat yellow spider rappelling down the side of the truck. (We carefully packed him up and set him in a safe place before driving away.)

Another spider's successful hunt—a big ant kicking futilely in a strand of sticky silk on the edge of the shed door. With a rather unpleasant sensation of godlike power I wonder whether I will help him get free. I decide against him and in favor of the spider and walk away, feeling a bit sadistic.

While walking across a hayfield that Ken is about to cut, Marilyn and I encounter a splendid, camouflage-suited mega-toad. I pick up this marvellous piece of toad-engineering to remove him to a safer place. And what safer place than the swampy edge of my front yard? I adopt him and Marilyn gets the job of holding him while I drive home. We free him in a damp depression in the tall grass outside the yard and leave him to regain his cool composure. No doubt he is furious about this unceremonious displacement from his old home. How can we tell him that we probably saved his life?

Actually, life consists of a lot of misunderstandings of good intentions. Just a minute ago, as I sat writing with my faithful Tim cat at my feet, he suddenly gave me a swift, claws-out bat across the ankle. Fool cat! Stop that! Then I discovered he was batting at the same mosquito I'd been trying to swat all evening.

JULY 3

Another inch and a half of rain fell overnight and today has been a glowering day of fierce black clouds being rolled across the sky by a racing wind. Two great blue herons flew into the cloudy sky, one rising off the river flat right in the middle of Sundre, and the other flying down the creek at home. Swallows swoop through the air like fighter planes, shooting down mosquitoes.

The horses accidentally got out into the hayfields so I had some healthful if unintentional exercise getting them home again. The woods are full of wildflowers. White seems to be the fashion this week. Wild strawberry blossoms, distinctive four-petalled, greenish-white bunchberry flowers, Dutch clover, northern bedstraw, a mass of solomon's seal along one bank of the creek, the opposite bank carpeted with white, mauve-veined wood violets. Wild geraniums are scattered through the woods, along with the occasional fuzzy white flower of the baneberry—so named because of its poisonous red berries. And in sunny meadows everywhere, the caraway blooms. It's not really a wildflower, I'm told, but a feral plant, introduced by Norwegian settlers to flavor their traditional dishes and now gone wild like a virulent virus, spreading white lace through the fields.

JULY 6

A day of thundershowers—ominous blue-black clouds, racing in, rumbling and grumbling, dumping sudden deluges and then racing off to find some new mischief. One managed to produce a funnel cloud at Airdrie, fifty miles away but, fortunately, no damage was done.

In the hush before one thunderstorm, a sound from the sky caught my attention. It is impossible to describe this eerie sound but the closest I can come is to compare it to a siren. Not the high-pitched, screaming kind but the alternating kind that bleat, recede into almost-silence and then bleat again. Since I was fairly sure I wasn't hearing a flying police car I assumed the sound must be made by a raven, that master of peculiar airborne noises. But as I scanned the sky, I was proven wrong as not one, but two, flying sirens winged heavily into view, as strange to the eye as they were to the ear. All necks and legs and awkwardness, it was a pair of great blue herons, making their way west from the beaver dam across the road. Never in all the times I've seen herons around have I heard one's voice. But then again, I've never seen a pair together before. Maybe it was sweet nothings they were calling to each other. From the tone of their voices I'm afraid it sounded more like they were having a domestic dispute.

JULY 7

After more rain overnight and several heavy showers today, the sun is, at last, shining on a brilliant green and clean earth. The yard seems actually to glow with the richness of color. Water-drop diamonds shine among the royal purple columbines while a new-hatched burnt-orange poppy lifts its eager face to the sunlight. The little creek, often bone-dry by this time of year, gurgles and chortles with the voice of a young river. In spite of the wet grass, the sun lures Timothy to make a stately inspection of the bushes and shrubs. Passing bees bumble busily. Missy alternates between lying at my feet and climbing onto the bench beside me, the better to help me.

I took Copper for a ride in the sunshine. While loping along the edge of the hayfield, we almost ran over a young, velvet-antlered white-tail who was sleeping in the tall hay. He was one surprised deer as he bounded up almost under Copper's feet and high-tailed it out of there.

Later, on the way home through the woods, a little white-tail doe stood unperturbed watching us go by.

JULY 11

At last, full summer is here. We're in the middle of a little heat wave—which means it's 85°F on the cool side of the house at high noon. This country doesn't really know the meaning of *hot.* It always cools down enough to sleep at night and in this shady yard it never really gets uncomfortable.

The birds seem to be enjoying the heat. Robins are everywhere but, surprisingly, it is the song of the chickadees, our traditional winter bird, that fills the air on this hot day.

Sadness crept into the brightness of this afternoon. My aunt brought Sally, her old calico cat, out to be buried on the farm. Sally had just run out of time. She was past fifteen and so sick she wouldn't eat any more so the kindest thing to do was to have her put to sleep. It always hurts so much to say good-bye to an animal that you love. Anyone who can think of them as "just animals" has never really known an animal or accepted its innocent, uncomplicated trust.

So we shed some tears for Sally—or for us, since Sally is at peace. She looked so relaxed, curled up like any sleeping cat. She sleeps now beneath the grass on the hillside above the little creek in a sunlit glade surrounded by young spruce trees. The sounds there are of whispering wind and gurgling water and there are birds and squirrels to stalk in her happy hunting ground. A little willow grows at the head of her grave and, at its foot, a single, pure pink wintergreen flower grows wild.

Goodbye, Sally. Sleep well. You lived your life surrounded by love and died the same way. Can any of us ask for more?

JULY 12

I rode Copper in the cool of the evening. The woods are deep and lush with green. Clover blooms everywhere, its scent sweet on the breeze while wild roses grow in a dozen shades of pink. The pea family is at its blooming peak. The earliest garden peas are in blossom, along with their wild cousins in the woods: purple vetch, wild sweet pea, the various loco weeds. In the shadiest part of the yard, the little patch of tiny, delicate twin flowers are just opening their miniature pink bells.

This morning Missy was busily barking at something in the woods, not an unusual occurrence. Five minutes later she was back, with a whole noseful of quills. Michael (who is working for me this summer) and I set to work with pliers and tweezers. Not a cooperative patient! That's the way it goes, Missy. A minute's fun and look what you get.

JULY 14

Two different bird adventures this hot day. I had picked Mom up at her place in town and was bringing her out for a visit when I had to put on the brakes for an adolescent robin who was parked right in the middle of the lane and not about to move. I don't know what his problem was, maybe a bit of vertigo on his first flight. He didn't seem hurt, or even stunned, but he still didn't move when I got out and picked him up. He was a handsome, bright-eyed child, sleeker and more mature-looking than many robins making their first flights. Only his size and a slight mottling of color showed him to be a juvenile.

I carried him to the house and put him in a shoebox, temporarily, so that I could at least bring the car on up to the house. Minutes later, when I opened the box to check on him, he was much livelier, so lively that he immediately bit my finger as hard as he could, which fortunately was not very hard. He was determined, though. He sat grimly hanging on for several seconds, giving me a chance to study him in detail. And to discover his tongue. I'd never noticed a bird's tongue before. His was bright orange, like his beak, and triangular. Not surprising, I suppose, since it has to fit into a triangular beak.

Finally he let go and made an effort to get away so I decided he was ready to get on with his life. I took him to a spruce thicket near where I'd found him and, with one hand, set him on a branch. (The other hand was occupied with capturing The Prince who had clued into the fact that we were having a magnificent bird adventure and trekked enthusiastically along behind.) Bird immediately flitted to another branch and mama bird was making excited noises from a nearby tree so, probably, that story had a happy ending. (I brought The Prince into the house where he happily sacked out in a cool corner for the next six hours, so young robin had a good head start on *him*, at least.)

The second bird was also a near-miss, airborne this time. On the way back to Sundre we were just turning the corner onto the north road when a great flapping of wings erupted in front of the car. A beautiful red-tailed hawk was laboring awkwardly across the road like an overloaded 747, trying desperately to gain altitude without dropping the fat gopher he had just swept up in his talons. He made it! Ma will be pleased when he comes home with pot roast for the family's supper!

July 15

A nice, hot day, interrupted by a tiny shower that would be a nuisance only if I had some hay down. Mine is still standing. Since I pasture the fields in the spring, it's a bit later than some. Some of the fields are going to be good, others are not what they should be since the hay has been standing with its toes in water ever since the frost went out. One unfortunate thing is that two stubble fields that were supposed to be plowed and planted with oats this spring were never planted at all. It was just too wet to get on them with machinery all spring. However, nature once again shows her determination to let nothing go to waste. Although a few weeds grew up in the unplanted land, most of it automatically reverted to grass and clover on its own and Ken was able to cut a small early crop of hay on these fields. Certainly better than nothing on land where, theoretically, nothing was growing.

Today, it was a ruffed grouse assuming she had the right-of-way on the lane, strutting slowly across, high-headed and proud. She had a right to be proud. Seconds later, the air exploded with wingbeats as her family of at least five half-grown youngsters took to the air behind her.

There was another visitor—a foreign cat. I heard The Prince shouting insults at him from down across the creek. (If any theory suggests that neutered toms don't fight, they haven't met these three. They are fiercely territorial and show travellers *no* hospitality.)

By the time I arrived on the scene the intruder had disappeared, but I did find The Prince. Not a mark on him, but obviously he finds fighting, or even heavy-duty screeching, too much for a hot summer day. Despite the fact that he's shed down to his elegant silk pajamas, His Highness was so hot and tired he was panting like a dog. I brought him home and gave him some cold milk, after which he went straight to bed in a cool corner for the rest of the day.

Some big, macho cat!

July 19

More rain! Another inch in the last couple of days. As I looked out into the damp, gray morning, a visitor appeared. A beautiful white-tail buck with big velvet antlers stepped out into the opening I've been clearing south of the yard. He cautiously sniffed the air in all directions, nibbled a few poplar leaves and slowly made his way back into the deep green forest.

I was still feeling quite honored to have been favored by that regal visit when, later this morning, I strolled out to the garden to discover a dozen pea vines and my biggest broccoli plant had been neatly nibbled. I don't know who did it but there was a clue: big deer tracks in the mud along the row.

Now is that any way for a visitor to behave?

July 20

Missy and I went down to see the cattle on the north quarter this evening. As soon as I got out of the truck, I was enveloped in a cloud of sweet perfume from the acres of Dutch clover blooming in the pasture. As I walked closer to the resting cattle the smell of cows mingled not unpleasantly with the clover, bringing with it memories of long-ago walks with my dad as we checked the cattle together.

New flowers are blooming here now, delicate lilac-colored harebells, yellow cinquefoil and the ones that fascinate me, the bull thistles, as Dad used to call them. Totally different from the rude and rowdy Canada thistles that invade the pastures and fields at home, these thistles grow only in this open country. Ground-huggers with no stems at all, and only mild prickles on their silvery leaves, the bull thistles have a huge, lavender flower, two or more inches across.

The cows are fat and happy. My last late-bloomer has produced a sleek and healthy bull calf. Thus ends the calving season, only five months after it began in February!

While I looked at flowers and cows, Missy had her own adventure, a wild romp with two cocky young coyotes who live in a creek-bank den and were, no doubt, out for an evening of gophering.

JULY 22

A perfect deck-sitting morning with warm sunshine and a gentle breeze. Half a dozen kinds of birdsong filter down through the spruce branches while iridescent turquoise dragonflies swoop through the air: environmentally friendly self-propelled pesticides!

In the flower beds, a new dynasty reigns, the queens of high summer. The last of the pure yellow day lilies set off the deep purple of the fluffy-headed-I-can't-find-out-what-they're-calleds, which in turn stand in brilliant contrast to the scarlet of the Maltese crosses. (At least I got *their* name right this time. Half the time I'm either calling them iron crosses or iron maidens!) Tall spikes of sky-blue delphinium stand high above their neighbors while the too-thick shirley poppies which seed themselves every year crowd like groupies around the feet of the last, huge deep-orange oriental poppy.

All the time I've been writing this, an athletic worm has been climbing an invisible silk thread all the way from the deck level to a spruce branch six feet above. I'm sure he must be a very bad fellow, and I suppose that if I was a gung-ho gardener I'd be hyperventilating my way to the nearest spray can of worm killer. But I'm not too excited. That whole treeful of chickadees should be able to dispatch one small green worm.

In the afternoon I went to a dinner concert in Calgary. Ian Tyson and Michael Martin Murphy, two country singers I really enjoy. But the best part was that the proceeds of the concert went to the Friends of the Old Man River, an environmental group that has been fighting the controversial Old Man River Dam. I know that there are always two sides to any issue and that dried out farmers in southern Alberta really need the water, but I still question the whole plan. For one thing, I'm not sure that irrigation is always the answer. There is some evidence that too much irrigation will eventually deposit enough salt to ruin the land. Maybe the problem is that people are trying to crop land that should never have been anything but pasture.

And my other reason for siding against the dam is that I don't believe that the government has the right to wreck the land in one area to improve it in another. I keep thinking about how I would feel if it was *this* land that was to be flooded to benefit somebody a hundred miles away. Losing your land is like losing a part of you. It hurts.

JULY 24

Took salt down to the cows on the north quarter. Much to Missy's delight, the place is alive with gophers, which soon have her running around like the rabbit in *Alice in Wonderland*. No matter how fast she goes, she's always just a little late. Just at the strategic moment, the little critters drop out of sight to hide safely in their burrows, only to reappear the instant she looks the other way.

But here, too, nature provides checks and balances. From a sunny hillside, two alert bandit-faces are watching us. Badgers, those rolling-gaited, consummate gopher hunters, have established a homestead of their own, right here in Gopherville.

JULY 26

Another damp morning after a night, a day and another night of showers. This weather encourages my natural lazy streak. As I idle over a second cup of coffee and a book about a family who owns an island, the animals idle with me. The Prince is on the couch, washing his pajamas after a night out on the country. Timothy, with his foot-fetish, lies cosily on my bare toes. Missy, on her rug by the door, lies with her nose on her fancy, Appaloosa-spotted front paw, regarding me with such love and trust that it makes me

almost sad. She seems so vulnerable. How can anyone betray the simple, unquestioning faith of animals?

As I write this, a new rain begins, and I need to go outside to borrow a toad for an hour to go with a story I'm supposed to tell at the town library.

At supper time the sun finally came out, brightening the western sky in contrast to the heavy, blue-black clouds that still dominated the east.

I took Copper and Missy out for a run. The Indian paintbrushes are in full bloom, flowers that really do look exactly like brushes daubed with every hue of paint: cream, honey, salmon, pink, fuschia, scarlet . . .

Along the road, the death camas grow in profusion this wet year. A delicate, silver-green stalk holds up a pure, greenish-white flower. It's supposed to be poisonous to livestock, but I don't get too excited about it. My wet, woodland pasture is full of poisonous plants: baneberry, larkspur, water hemlock. I suppose that, over the years, an occasional animal has been lost, but generally, when the grass is good, the animals won't bother with the exotic stuff. (They seem to be a bit brighter than the human race, which is prone to taking almost any sort of substance into its body just to see what will happen!) Anyway, the poisonous plants are just another part of the ecosystem here. We manage to coexist.

I never did find a toad this morning. All I got for my search was wet. But as I walked up to the front porch tonight a movement caught my eye: a big, handsome toad not two feet from the door. Where were you when I needed you, toad?

JULY 27

A cloudy morning, brightened by a breakfast invitation from the neighbors. Missy and I walked the half mile, pausing for an appetizer in a patch of wild strawberries along the lane. The Prince followed along a little while. After lunch I found him down by the creek where he'd stopped off for a morning's exploration. I'd often wondered if he bothered to come around by the bridge when he wanted to cross the creek. He certainly doesn't. When I called him from the other side of the water he strolled up to the bank and effortlessly sailed four feet through the air to land on the bank beside me.

This evening it turned cloudy again but I resisted the urge to be a couch potato and took Copper out for a four-mile ride. He got his first shoes a couple of weeks ago so now I can ride him on the road. The only things out there he found scary enough to shy at were some clumps of flowers. Does this mean I have a horse related to Ferdinand, Walt Disney's bull with the delicate ego?

Copper does have a great memory, though. Almost exactly two years ago I bought him from Ron Gale, a horse trainer and trader who lives on the next road west. Copper was just two when he left Ron's place and he hasn't been back since. But tonight when I rode past Ron's gate the horse was determined that he should turn in there.

We encountered some interesting wildlife along the way: two deer, one mule and one white-tail, and a mother grouse with her half-grown brood.

Speaking of wildlife, I have a squirrel in the barn that must have biceps like Sylvester Stallone. I keep a paint can full of oats in the tack room to give my horse a treat while I'm saddling up and whenever I finish with it, I pound the lid on with my fist. But, every time I go to get oats, the lid is off and I have more hulls than oats left. To add insult to injury, the brush-tailed bandit was grinning down at me from a roof beam tonight.

JULY 28

The summer's hit horror movie is *Arachnaphobia*. So should I feel a little tense when I discover a full dozen huge, identical spiders exploring my back step?

No panic attack, since I didn't see the movie.

JULY 29

I began this sunny, breezy day by sitting on the deck listening to the cheerful crowing of the neighbors' rooster, a mile down the road, and watching the busy robins who have nested just across the lane.

Supper was a wiener roast with Walkers, one of the few in history not interrupted by rain. Then a walk up to the big beaver dam. Today's denizens-in-residence included two families of fluffy, half-grown ducks, a snipe, a kingfisher and three tail-slapping beavers. The walk continued to the hayfield where the hay was better than I'd expected, but still standing with its toes in water in some places.

Wet-footed, we came home, and encountered neighbors out for an evening walk down the road. We all came in, stirred up the campfire, boiled up another potful of cowboy coffee and visited in the friendly circle of firelight till the fire was just an island of glowing embers in the darkness.

JULY 30

I'm stealing a little reading time on the deck with the chickadees bugging in the tree above me and nuthatches yiking happily below the hill. On the lower lawn, the robin forages for her bottomless brood. It's fascinating to have their nest so close to the house, but I don't think putting it here was a very smart move on the birds' behalf, not with three cats in residence. But right now the robin has nothing to fear. Two cats are fast asleep here on the deck. And there's not much danger from fat, old, three-legged Tim, wherever that nimrod is.

A short walk in the south woods yields wild fruit salad: several wild currants, a handful of dewberries and one huge wild strawberry. I also came upon a beautiful wild fern, something rare around here. Also, blessedly rare this wet year, a wasp. The first one I've seen all summer. He caught my attention by the scratching sound he was making, scraping wood pulp from a rotten stump. His tribe are probably the only environmentally safe paper mills, safe as long as you keep your distance from their paper houses!

JULY 31

A beautiful morning and early afternoon, most of which I wasn't able to enjoy because this was carpet-cleaning day. Once the machine is rented there's no way to postpone the tedious task! I never know if I've actually got the carpet clean, but judging from the water I threw out there are definitely several less pailsful of mud in it than when I started.

Right in the middle of all that mess the well driller came to drill a new back-up well for the cattle up by the barn.

About five-thirty a big thunderstorm rumbled up. Not a violent one. The thunder and lightning were quite distant but the water supply was plentiful. Three years ago today, twenty-seven people died in the infamous Edmonton tornado, so I guess we should gracefully accept our mere rainstorms.

As soon as the rain stopped, Missy and I set out on a long walk to enjoy the cool, clean-smelling evening. This wet weather is encouraging some far-out plants to emerge. In the north woods I spotted an orange fungus that looked like it should have been a sponge or coral growing on some tropical reef. Who knows, if this weather keeps up long enough, the dinosaurs may make a comeback.

AUGUST 2

I encountered one of nature's masterpieces today, a caterpillar designed to impersonate a poplar twig. Smooth, grayish-green skin, little joint ridges. The only giveaway was that this twig walked like an inchworm, on five sets of legs, three in front and two behind.

AUGUST 3

After another couple of days of showers, today was perfect.

Bird images define the day:

Trees full of busy, singing chickadees in the early morning.

A family of bluebirds swooping across the road like small, bright-painted airplanes.

A weary but proud robin sitting in her nest tree, beak overflowing with worms for the kids.

At sunset, flights of crows heading home to roost across a purple sky.

AUGUST 6

Ten o'clock on a warm summer night. A full, golden moon climbs slowly through the branches of the eastern trees. The tireless robin makes one last trip to the supermarket to get pureed worms for the insatiable brood. A coyote chorus sings a few bars. Somewhere in the deep dark woods, *something* calls, beginning with a sort of moo and ending with a throat gargle. An animal? A bird? Or some unspeakable monster, lurking, waiting. . .

If I was a writer like Stephen King or Dean R. Koontz, the first chapter of my next book would be half written. But, I'm afraid I might scare *myself* to death so I guess I'll just forget the idea for the time being. Actually, I think I would prefer to write horror stories the same way I like to read them—at ten o'clock in the morning surrounded by quarrelling chickadees and blazing sunshine.

Now it is Missy's turn to get a scare. As she lies near me on the deck, a big jet rumbles its way out of the southern sky, waking her from a deep sleep. Instantly her ears stand up, then the rest of her stands up, wide awake and tingling with apprehension. "Thunderstorm alert!" she signals, hurrying over to me and insisting that we should both take shelter in the house at once. While she's still trying to get this information through my thick head, the jet has crossed the sky and is already droning away into silence in the northern sky. Just like any person who has made a bit of a fool of herself, Missy gives a dog shrug, turns around, and flops down beside me with kind of an embarrassed sigh, pretending she just came over to say hello and now will get on with her nap.

The last couple of days are what summer is supposed to be. Hot, sunny, all the earth green and fruitful under a dazzling blue canopy. Just enough breeze to keep the heat from being oppressive. Wonderful days. Yet, in a way, they make me sad. Again, Robert Frost's poem, "Nothing Gold Can Stay." Summer, like life, is so fleeting. I want to grab these days, squeeze them, milk out their essence and store it away in a jar, a magic potion to stave off encroaching winter.

AUGUST 7

Wasted half an hour this morning hunting for The Prince who was late for breakfast. Missy had a big, alarmed barking jag at something very near the house last night so, of course, I again began imagining that His Majesty had been eaten in one great gulp. (Possibly by the monster that called in the woods last night?)

So I trudged twice to the barnyard, calling Pr-i-i-i-nce, like an idiot. Morris and Timothy eagerly presented themselves for admiration. Missy came walloping up, tongue hanging out. Four hospitable horses followed me through their pasture, stepping on my heels and blowing warm, clover-scented breath down my neck. A wonderful menagerie. But was I satisfied? No! Like the shepherd in the Bible with ninety-nine sheep in the fold, I still had to find my lost one.

At last, hot and weary, I trudged back up the lane to the house. There on the shady deck sat The Prince, elegant and cool, washing his silk pajamas as he waited for me to come and let him in for breakfast.

Between that cat and me, it's not hard to choose the more intelligent life-form.

The Prince not only came for breakfast this morning, he *brought* breakfast! He came scurrying into the house, around the corner, and out to the feeding dishes so fast and unobtrusively that I didn't notice he was carrying a package. Not until I found all three cats crouched admiringly around the fine, fat, freshly-killed young squirrel he had deposited beside his dish. Needless to say, I removed it quite quickly to the lawn. I'm not sure who finally ate it but nothing was wasted. One tuft of burnt-sienna tail hair was all that remained by noon.

I always feel a little badly when the cats catch squirrels but, there again, is the balance of nature. These woods are full of squirrels and if all the young ones lived to grow up they'd over-populate until they starved to death.

I think this is leaving-home season for the young squirrels because a lot of small, foolish ones seem to be around these days. Another one almost met his Waterloo with Missy this afternoon. In a yard full of spruce trees this young fool for some reason insisted on taking a run across the widest part of the open grass. Of course Missy was instantly in hot pursuit. By the skin of his teeth, the squirrel made it into the shelter of a willow, barely eight feet tall, then jumped into a still-smaller one, only to find himself clinging uncomfortably to a very flexible branch-tip. Poor fellow was stuck there for half the afternoon while Missy, beside herself with excitement at being this close to actually sinking her teeth into one of those chittering varmints, paraded back and forth in the hot sun like a sentry in the French Foreign Legion, determined that the enemy would *not* escape. But he did. The dog finally got tired and retired to the shade under the deck. I saw the squirrel ease down from his perch and hightail it (literally) for the nearest tree.

So, the score today was a tie. Domestic Critters—1. Squirrels—1.

Today was also graduation day for the robins. The kids flew the coop! I've been watching them all evening as, one at a time, they make their way out of the nest and onto nearby branches to receive a wormy reward from their proud parents. One young one is still in the nest tree, one has already made his first flight over to the willow. I've lost track of the third, who must have moved out before I noticed what was going on. Fortunately there are no cats on deck just now, and these seem to be pretty bright children. If they can survive the next couple of days of flight lessons they should be on their way. Then their parents, looking a little ruffled and worn like a lot of parents of adolescents, can breathe a deep sigh of relief and start planning a Florida vacation.

AUGUST 8

Definitely a spider year! Webs everywhere. On the corner of the deck railing, one huge mama crouches in the corner of her web, waiting. Suddenly, a good-sized fly is caught. With the deceptive speed of a heavyweight wrestler, Big Mama skitters down the web, grabs her victim in a body scissors and carries him back to the pantry corner. Then, lying on her back, she begins to twirl the fly with her feet, like a beach ball, encasing it in a cocoon of silk. Neatly packaged, he is stored away by the provident old spider with her other preserves, food for a rainy day. It's too bad so many people can't seem to manage this level of planning.

Some kind of a mega-mosquito is being preserved on the other side of the deck. This creature hangs suspended in a drop of spruce sap from the umbrella tree that shades the deck. (This tree is impartial with regard to species. More than once it has also tried to preserve me in its sticky sap, sometimes resulting in an impromptu haircut to remove a big, gooey gob from the back of my head.)

Now, I wonder what will become of this mosquito. A million years from now, will someone unearth a piece of amber with this primitive 1990 life-form perfectly preserved within?

I knew it would happen. The slowest of the robin children made a flight from the nest tree while I was on the deck this morning. Unfortunately for the bird, The Prince, keeping me company, was nearby. My back was turned so I missed the opening sequence of this drama but suddenly I heard great wing rustlings and chirpings. At some hazard to life and limb, I plunged down the deck stairs in time to see The Prince running across the lawn with the flapping baby in his mouth, hotly pursued by its two screaming parents. I threw myself into the fray, yelling at The Prince to put it down, and succeeding in arousing Missy, who came walloping around the corner to see what wonderful sport she was missing. It was a miracle that neither one of us managed to trample the poor bird in our enthusiasm. Finally, I got it away from the cat, apparently unhurt. I stuck it back into the nest tree, whereupon it promptly fluttered back to the ground. Another narrow rescue! This time I carried the dimwitted child to a group of spruces by the creek, all the while being divebombed by dad who did not seem to understand the nature of my good deed.

I scooped up The Disappointed Prince under my arm, called Missy and headed for the house. Sort it out, birds. I've done my part.

AUGUST 12

Hot summer days. How can anything so lazy unroll and disappear so quickly into the never-to-be-recaptured past? I spend time in the mornings down at the campsite by the creek. Time I should spend cleaning my dusty bedroom. But I have no guilt. That is drudgery. This is living. Missy and The Prince come with me to share this spot of sun-dappled shade. Birds share it, too. Chickadees fill the trees in the early morning. Nuthatches, woodpeckers, a yellow warbler or two and, today, the first pair of whisky jacks I've seen in weeks. A squirrel, the master of aerial ballet, passes by twenty feet above our heads, needing no trail but the spreading branches.

Now the horses come to visit, wading the little creek to graze in the arm of the pasture that comes up just across the fence. One horse stops in the creek to bathe. A marvellous trick in hot buggy weather. She stands knee-deep in the water and paws it violently to a muddy froth, splashing it all over herself, drenching and cooling her itchy hide. Missy disapproves of all the noise, however, and runs over barking, causing a minor stampede and spoiling all the fun.

Missy's own punishment is swift in coming, though. The Prince rises lazily from a catnap in the cool grass and, of course, the dog can't resist going over to pester him a little. There is a sudden anguished yelp. I look up. Sure enough, Missy's black rubber nose has been punctured again!

But even with these idyllic summer days comes a melancholy reminder of autumn waiting just around the corner. As I sit here among the young balsam poplars, an occasional dry leaf drifts down through their greenness to lie curled and dead on the ground. When I rode through the woods this week—a ride which, incidentally, brought me close to a beautiful cow elk grazing on the hillside, her coffee-and-cream hide glowing in the late-day sun—I found small forest shrubs already turning their bottom leaves to clear lemon yellow.

The wildflowers now are from the end-of-summer purple palette. Wild asters and daisy fleabane in pale lilac shades, deep-purple larkspur, orchidlike mauve flowers on the hedge nettle, pink-purple ones on the obnoxious hemp nettle, fluffy mauve blossoms on the *extremely* obnoxious Canada thistle. Everywhere, graceful spikes of tall, magenta fireweed, classed as a weed only because it's so common. If fireweed was hard to grow, gardeners across the country would be pampering it in flower beds.

Among the tame flowers, most of the perennials are finished. The slow and stately monkshood blooms in splendid solitude while petunias and asters blaze their pinks and purples from the annual bed.

AUGUST 13

A beautiful bright and shiny morning with a fresh breeze promising to temper the day's heat and help dry the day. Yes, haying is *finally* under way with the first fields yielding excellent crops in spite of, and because of, the spring deluges. Rich green windrows, too wide to step across, snake their way across the fields, filling the air with the exotic aroma of drying hay. I've always thought the perfume companies have missed out on a sure thing by not coming out with a fragrance called "New-Mown Hay."

One sad note in the haying yesterday. We had to shoot a porcupine that Ken accidentally hit with the swather while the porky was hiding in the tall hay. So many animals are the innocent victims of our technology. We devise faster and more efficient ways to get the job done and the poor critters are literally mown down in our path. I don't suppose many people would mourn the passing of a porky, probably considering him a nuisance happily eliminated. But, despite all of Missy's mishaps with them, I don't hate the porkies. They aren't malicious. They just bumble along living their quiet life and picking no quarrels. And as for the dogs' pincushioned noses, if *we* were being molested by an animal twice our size, wouldn't we give it a good slap with the only weapon we had?

AUGUST 14

Another hot haying day. At dusk I drive up to count today's bales. In the pasture field a mule deer doe grazes in knee-deep Dutch clover, looking up with only mild interest as my Hollywood-mufflered (read that holes-in-the-mufflered) truck rambles past.

From the top of the hill field the countryside spreads out, its outlines softened by deep-summer haze. In the distance, a couple of farmyard lights send out their friendly glow. Close at hand, green fields, some still deep with uncut hay, others with windrows braided across them, still others flaunting the neat silver-green loaves of round bales, all packaged and ready for winter.

AUGUST 19

A weather change. Nearly an inch and a half of rain in the last couple of days and I'm sitting on the covered boardwalk watching more rain fall this evening. Two days ago, the little creek had just dried up for the first time all summer. Now it runs full and singing again. The grass and trees shine a clean bright green and the air smells wonderful. There's just one catch: I've got *hay* down again. Visions of last year's black bales come back to haunt me. (Bales which, incidentally, the cows not only ate but thrived on, coming through the winter fat and sassy with bright and healthy calves. It scares me to think what a nutritional analysis of that hay might have told me. Sometimes ignorance really is bliss.)

AUGUST 20

Between the weekend's rain and the prediction of more rain to come, today was beautiful. Just warm enough to be comfortable and with a breeze to blow the flies away.

I took Copper out for a long ride this evening to the end of the west quarter and then a winding tour home again, exploring the creek. Its course has always been determined by the vagaries of the resident beavers. Dams come and go. Where a whole lake spreads out one year, the next year there is only a narrow channel surrounded by a mud flat and a new lake appears up or downstream, wherever the food supply strikes the beavers' fancy.

A drained-out dam has grown up with tall slough grass. A coyote surprised by our intrusion lopes away, only a pair of ears visible, seeming to skim along above the swaying grass on their own propulsion. Above a new, water-filled dam, a kingfisher makes his effortless flights. Nearby a family of a half-dozen teenage grouse bursts into the air with a sudden whir of heavy wings.

In the woods, royal colors are in fashion now. Purple asters massed against a bank of goldenrod. (Is it really goldenrod? I'm not sure. Golden-something, anyway.)

In the yard, my yellow tea rose finally unfurls its creamy petals while the sweet peas, the first really successful ones I've ever grown, make fragrant rainbows along the house. The old hop vine that I rescued from my great aunt's deserted yard drips cascades of fuzzy hops around the deck railing. (I've had quite a struggle with that old vine this year. He's grown with such enthusiasm that I've had to guide his curling tendrils with a firm hand. He keeps reaching out to wrap them around the necks of the blushing young petunias. Dirty old vine!)

AUGUST 21

A day that couldn't make up its mind. Cool and cloudy. Then, suddenly bright and hot. Then, threatening a thunderstorm. Clear and calm at bedtime.

At last, a reason for the existence of the obnoxious Canada thistles. In the barnyard today, two wonderful black-trimmed, lemon-yellow goldfinches, shining brighter than sunlight as they flit from thistle to thistle, dining on the new-ripened seeds. And, if you can get past the prickles to smell them, thistles *do* have a sweeter smell than the most genteel of garden flowers.

AUGUST 23

Yesterday the weather didn't know what to do. It rained early in the morning, then suddenly blew away all the clouds and scoured the sky to a sunshiny blue at noon. By evening, an armada of fierce-looking thunderclouds did war maneuvers across the sky, rumbling, clashing, sweeping together to form impenetrable walls of gray, suddenly parting like the Red Sea to show enough blue to make a Dutchman a pair of breeches. (This has always been my mother's criterion for judging weather. If there's that much blue, it won't rain. But, she's never been too clear on the size of the Dutchman. I've seen some pretty big ones!)

This morning dawned (it was so dark and gray that I hesitate to say it dawned at all) cold, cloudy and with misting rain. It feels like a prologue to fall. Already the horses have lost their super-slick summer look. They're still sleek and shiny but the first layer of longer hair is growing in.

The weather was too much for The Prince this morning. If he'd have been a kid I'd have been counting the seconds till school started. For his first act, immediately after breakfast he hurried over and jumped on old Morris who, as usual, was sleeping. Pleased at having disturbed the old fellow, The Prince then announced he was ready to go outside. Half an hour later, underwear and fur slippers dripping wet, His Majesty arrived on the outside windowsill, demanding to come in and leaving wet-fur smears on the glass. In again, he picked a fight with Timothy, stood on a chair and put his wet front paws on the table (I stopped that little exercise before the rest of the cat could join the paws) and then finished his performance by leaving muddy pussy-paw marks all over the pink chair cover in the living room.

Then he smiled benignly and went to sleep.

A desolate evening. Dark, sullen clouds brooding heavily over a solemn land. A feeling of snow in the cold damp air. Like a winter evening but without the hope of spring around the corner. All the sadness of the world hangs heavy on such a night. Time to build a good fire in the stove to warm body and soul and seek solace in the touch of warm fur and the company of contented animals.

AUGUST 27

Monday, after a damp, cold, gloomy weekend that I missed. Marilyn and I drove 400 miles north to the Grande Prairie country to visit old friends, Art and Ruth. It's always a surprise to rediscover just how big and empty Alberta really is. Miles and miles of untouched forest from just north of Edmonton until the farming country of the Peace River area opens out again.

Those untouched trees drive the politicians crazy. With visions of dollar signs dancing through their heads they drool over possibilities of new pulp mills. But as far as I can see, those "waste" lands are doing just fine the way they are. They're sheltering wildlife and producing oxygen, a role not unlike that of the endangered rain forests. Why can't we just leave those woods alone and let them get on with their work? The world was never meant to be paved.

AUGUST 28

Missy got herself into a bit of trouble last night. Just after I had gone to bed there was a sudden, injured yelp from outside. I hurried to the door, expecting she'd been attacked by a passing grizzly, or at least had another noseful of quills. But her only injury was a thin bleeding scratch above her eyebrow. Mysterious! Finally, rightly or wrongly, I laid the blame at The Prince's door. A war game that got a little rough? I let Missy in to have a better look at the damage. Unable to reach the spot for the traditional dog first-aid of licking the wound, she resourcefully does the next best thing: bends down and wipes the blood off on her sleeping rug, then neatly licks the rug off. I conclude that she will live, but leave her in to avoid yet another outdoor commotion. We all go to sleep, except, perhaps, The Prince. He has made himself extremely scarce throughout the incident.

August 29

These last days of summer may be its most beautiful. The nights have grown cold, the temperature teetering dangerously on the edge of frost, but the mornings dawn glorious blue with air like fine crystal. The dew is like an overnight rain. When The Prince came charging across the lawn for breakfast, his magnificent tail waving on high like a cavalry banner, a spray of water flew up from the grass with every bound. This wetness slows the haying. Nothing can be done in the fields until noon, at the earliest.

The morning sun is later now. At eight-thirty I sit here at the campsite in the first warm patch of sunlight, drinking coffee that steams in the cool air. The sounds of the countryside surround me. Half a mile away, a cow gives forth with a long series of calf-calling bawls. Across the road, a duck quacks. Above me, the trees are alive with motion and the cheerful voices of foraging chickadees. A distant crow caws. As fast-talking as an auctioneer, a squirrel spiels off an opinion. A single dry leaf falls crisply through the branches. The creek gurgles. Nuthatches peep tunelessly. A horse coughs, reminding me to shut them out of the hay corral where they've discovered a musty old bale to nose in, despite the fact that the grass is still knee-high in their pasture.

August 30

I woke to the patter of little feet this morning: a squirrel galloping around on the roof. This, plus the raucous cries of the blue jays, made sure I stayed awake. Just as well, since it was already seven-thirty. It was still gray outside, though. The days have begun their ever-accelerating plunge toward the equinox, and on to the darkness of winter.

But winter is not a thought for today. Today the sun is shining and the grass is green. I sit at the campsite, burning shingle wrappings in the fire pit and listening to Michael, busily shingling my garage roof. Half a mile north, an ancient John Deere putt-putts as my neighbor Jim saws wood with his good old-fashioned buzz saw. What does all this activity mean? That it's time *I* got busy with something useful, too, particularly since I'm off to the dentist in an hour.

AUGUST 31

Walked up to the big beaver dam this evening. It's not at its best this time of year. A bit scummy and stagnant after the hot days of summer. Saw no beavers but their presence is very much in evidence: the wretched creatures have been toying with damming up my culvert where the trail crosses the creek!

I did see four happy ducks, paddling around in the soupy water, upending every now and then for an underwater tidbit. Are ducks really happy? They have a happy look on their faces. These had a huge swimming pond, lots to eat and each other, so I suppose they were happy. I think animals are happy for the most part, if they have the basic essentials of life. Much more so than humans.

These were nondescript dowdy-brown ducks, maybe juveniles not yet decked out in adult plumage, or else all females. Why is it that, in the animal world, the females are nondescript and the males have to run around in their expensive outfits knocking themselves out to impress them, while in the human world it's the females who are supposed to be beautiful but nonetheless attracted to any paunchy old executive who happens to have a little power and money? Somewhere the system got severely discombobulated, I fear.

SEPTEMBER 1

Signs of approaching winter! This morning, Morris emerged warm and sleepy from the dog's house where the two of them spent the night curled up together. Timothy came in, ate breakfast and immediately lumbered over to lie down with his huge belly completely covering a heat register. He does this regularly in the winter.

No wonder my propane bill is high, what with that tub of lard insisting on absorbing all the heat. Down at the campsite, the sprinkling of fallen leaves is quickly turning into a deep-pile carpet.

A squirrel is nipping off cones and letting them fall to the ground but stopping to eat about every third one instead of letting it drop. (I can identify with this squirrel. That's how I operate while preparing meals, too!)

Some cones fall to the deck with a loud crack, reminding me of a story my friend Lynne once brought back from a trip to the eastern United States. She and her friend had parked the camper in a campground near Washington, D.C., and, from a park warden, received a firm lecture on the dangers of walking around the city after dark. After all these warnings, they went to bed a little tense that night. Suddenly, they were awakened by a gunshot. Too scared to get up and investigate, they lay listening. Minutes passed. Another shot! Then another! All through the night, they huddled miserably, listening to the sporadic gun battle. Thoroughly shaken by morning, they arose at first light and crept outside to look for signs of carnage. There were none. The campground drowsed in perfect peace. Then, as they stood looking around in bewilderment, an acorn from the giant oak above them came plummeting down to bounce off the camper's metal top.

SEPTEMBER 3

Labor Day. The end of the last long weekend of summer. Tomorrow, summer holidays officially end and life becomes disciplined as school starts again. But not for me! I'm on leave of absence this year and tonight I think I can almost identify with those convicts who get last-minute pardons from the electric chair.

It's not that I won't miss school. I will miss it, the same way you miss the pain of hitting your head on the wall after you stop doing that. Dickens could have been talking about the teaching business when he began *A Tale of Two Cities*, "It was the very best of times; it was the very worst of times." No experience is more wonderful than when a kid suddenly turns on to learning. No experience is more mind numbing than sitting through a two-hour staff meeting on a hot September afternoon, discussing the supervision schedule and other items of earth-shaking importance.

Tonight after supper I rode Copper up to look at the hay. It's all baled! And the bales are all a beautiful, sweet-smelling silver-green. Not a black one in the bunch.

September 9

The year has come full circle. On a sunny Sunday last September I began this journal. Now, on another sunny Sunday, I sit amid the falling leaves absorbing the aura of autumn and trying to weave together the strands of the year into a tapestry of my life here.

The Prince is on my lap, Missy at my feet. Birds sing overhead. A light fog rises as the sun warms the cool but still unfrosted earth.

The hay is baled.

The cows are home, earlier than last year because a new beaver dam made their old creek-crossing down in the summer pasture impassable and so almost half of the north quarter remained untouched. But with all the rain, the cattle did well on the part they did graze, and the grass at home is plentiful.

The yellow warblers are back in my chokecherry bush, joined this year by some enterprising robins, eager to share the spoils. The robins have changed from the bedraggled and harassed parents of early August. Sleek, fat and unhurried now, they remind me of the retired people who drive placidly around in big motor homes with out-of-province licence plates.

A flicker has moved into the neighborhood, or is possibly just passing through on a migration. I love these big, friendly, flamboyant relatives of the woodpeckers. The flicker's main color is a sort of tawny brown, which is lavishly decorated with a white spot on the back, red neck (good, true backwoods Albertan!) and gold-to-salmon edged wings, which fan out in a beautiful burst of color as he flies.

A raucous cry overhead interrupts my train of thought as I sit here at the campsite by the creek, writing this farewell entry. I look up, expecting to see a raven, and find that I have much more exotic visitors. Out of nowhere, a great blue heron flaps slowly overhead to land in a spruce not a hundred feet away. There he sits, neck bent into a question mark, silhouetted against the sun. A minute later, his mate flies in to join him, landing out of sight in a lower tree. With storklike movements, heron number one proceeds to preen himself, muttering hoarsely as he works. Minutes later, a squawk announces takeoff, and with a few more calls to each other the pair flaps off to the east, following the creek back into the wild quarter across the road.

I try to round up my stray thoughts and bring them back to my year-end tapestry. But then I realize that moments like this, when organized thoughts give way to the everyday wonders that are a part of life on the land, are what give living here its texture and color. That's what it's all about, the reliable, unchanging cycles, interspersed with each day's small, unheralded miracles.

Was it a good year? How do you judge? The spring was so wet that the greenfeed didn't get planted, but the pasture grew like never before and hay is plentiful all over the country. The slugs and the deer got most of the garden peas that didn't drown first, but great banks of sweet peas are still spreading clouds of color and fragrance along the house. Nature's game of give and take.

Yes, it was a good year. All things bright and beautiful came in their season to be seen and shared by those who took the time to look. Now, another winter looms ahead.

But in six months new calves will be playing in the spring sunshine . . .